THE LEARNING TREE

THE LEARNING TREE

*Overcoming Learning Disabilities
from the Ground Up*

Stanley I. Greenspan, M.D.
and
Nancy Thorndike Greenspan

With contributions by
Richard Lodish, Ed.D., associate headmaster,
Sidwell Friends School

A Merloyd Lawrence Book
DA CAPO PRESS/LIFELONG BOOKS

Designed by Trish Wilkinson
Set in 12 point Goudy by the Perseus Books Group

Library of Congress Cataloging-in-Publication Data

Greenspan, Stanley I.
    The learning tree : overcoming learning disabilities from the ground up / Stanley I. Greenspan and Nancy Thorndike Greenspan ; with contributions by Richard Lodish. — 1st Da Capo Press ed.
       p. cm.
    "A Merloyd Lawrence Book."
    Includes bibliographical references and index.
    ISBN 978-0-7382-1233-3 (alk. paper)
    1. Learning disabilities—Prevention. 2. Slow learning children—Education (Early childhood)—Activity programs. 3. Children with disabilities—Education. I. Greenspan, Nancy Thorndike. II. Title.
LC4704.G735 2010
371.9'043—dc22   2010014225

First Da Capo Press edition 2010

A Merloyd Lawrence Book
Published by Da Capo Press
A Member of the Perseus Books Group
www.dacapopress.com

Da Capo Press books are available at special discounts for bulk purchases in the U.S. by corporations, institutions, and other organizations. For more information, please contact the Special Markets Department at the Perseus Books Group, 2300 Chestnut Street, Suite 200, Philadelphia, PA, 19103, or call (800) 810-4145, ext. 5000, or e-mail special.markets@perseusbooks.com.

10 9 8 7 6 5 4 3 2 1

To the thousands of children who have flourished because of the developmental insights of Stanley Greenspan . . . and to the thousands and thousands more who will do so in the future.
With love, Nancy

Contents

PART FOUR: THE BRANCHES

THE LEARNING TREE

Marilyn Nolt

Introduction

The Learning Tree

Surprise, anticipation, pleasure—eyes wide with excitement, mouth round with amazement, bright giggles in the air. These are the moments of wondrous discovery in a young child's life.

Children love to learn. From the first minute of their day, learning saturates every pulse. Their senses stand alert and eager to absorb more. At every opportunity, they seek out new encounters and challenges. They want more and more of whatever will expand their world. Children want to learn.

Yet, for many children, this zest does not endure. Once in school, they fiddle, they squirm, they whisper to friends, they do whatever they can not to pay attention—and not to learn. What switch flipped? What change made these adventurous little beings seemingly less curious, especially as their world becomes more complex and fascinating?

In the past, schoolchildren learned mostly by repetition and drilling, hardly the thrilling moments of their younger years. Mishaps often brought a stinging rap across the knuckles. More recently, educators gained the insight to focus on some basic abilities needed for reading and writing, such as figuring out sound patterns and basic motor skills. When these techniques took center stage, children nudged a little closer to their own natural style of learning, but for many children, their earlier wonderment and curiosity about the ever-expanding world still fade.

If you sense this happening in your child or in children in your classroom, we hope that the new approach presented in this book will reignite their excitement and joy in learning.

The research that led to this new approach began in 1975 when a group of pediatricians, child psychiatrists, and psychologists came together to discuss intellectual and emotional growth in early childhood. The pioneers—Berry Brazelton, Reg Lourie, Selma Fraiberg, and Ed Zigler among them—and the then-younger generation (myself included) wanted to launch a new era in understanding young children. The pioneers had begun the foundation for this understanding. Fraiberg's *The Magic Years* gave nascent insight into how children's knowledge grew, for instance how they learned to recognize patterns and how they acquired logic. But even so, the notion of babies and young children as little adults still permeated public perception.

The work of our group had to begin at the beginning—that is, with infants. When we explained the purpose of our research to other developmental experts, the response was often, "What emotional or cognitive problems can babies have?"

Our initial goal was to map the fundamental building blocks of children's emotional and intellectual development. Along with many of my colleagues, I've spent the intervening years trying to understand how healthy development progresses and why problems can occur. Now we have some answers. Once we saw how the fundamentals fit together, we could see what children need, whatever their age, and could identify for an individual child which of the basic building blocks have to be strengthened. (Please note: first-person pronouns in the general text refer to Dr. Stanley Greenspan.)

The Learning Tree draws on these many years of research. Because of this legacy, it takes a developmental perspective. Going beyond basic academic skills and even underlying abilities, such as recognizing sound and shapes used for reading, we show how the learning abilities themselves develop.

A developmental approach to learning takes into account all of a child's senses and his motor system. Most important, it recognizes the role of emotions in using and integrating these natural gifts. In early development, it is emotions that lead a child to use what he sees, hears, smells, tastes, and touches as well as to plan movement. Emotions start off as a physiological system receiving input from the senses. Then, through interpersonal experience, they drive a child's interest in the world and create an internal mental life. In other words, his emotions are the "orchestra leader" for the other parts of his mind. Understanding how emotions shape a child's mind into an integrated whole is the key to the developmental approach.

A developmental approach can expand the potential for all of us because all of us have strengths and weaknesses in our intellectual abilities no matter how high our IQs. Take Albert Einstein. He avoided speaking English because he could not speak it well, even though he lived in an English-speaking country for more than twenty years. One of the most brilliant minds ever could not master a skill that many of the most ordinary German refugees accomplished with little effort. Given the trade-off, we would all probably like to have Einstein's problem. If our children were discovering relativity, we would not sweat the small stuff such as learning a second language. But Einstein's difficulty with foreign languages certainly makes the point that there are always weaknesses, even in a genius. When abilities develop, new neural pathways form in the brain. Biology is not destiny if we detect problems early and give children extra practice with those skills that don't come easily.

Children who seem academically bewildered or whose curiosity seems to have shut down can reawaken their early joy and excitement. In our developmental approach, children's own innate ways of acquiring knowledge—ones that they have practiced since first turning to look at a parent—form the basis for their future learning. By observing how children's ways of learning build and expand through our decades of research, we have drawn a developmental "map" that describes the growth of fundamental abilities on which are built such critical, overriding skills as thinking and problem-solving. For children who appear to have lost their way in school, our understanding of this developmental process lets us pinpoint a step the child may have missed and focus on building this step to solidify the foundation.

It all begins simply—even with what are ultimately very difficult educational pursuits—because each new nugget of knowledge builds on an earlier one. Just take learning to read. As our group and others have seen, infants quickly learn to recognize the different sounds their caregivers make. They then construct patterns out of these sounds, and as they mature, they use these to decipher spoken and eventually written words. Our map shows how words come to have meaning: how babies and toddlers come to understand what the word "love" means or how words like "want" and "need" are similar, yet different. Insight into this process allows us not only to raise every child's reading comprehension but also to help him understand language more deeply. Our map of these and the many other steps in between enables us to help any struggling child become a better and more effortless reader. It's all in knowing how to lessen weaknesses and complement strengths.

Similarly, our map for building mathematical and scientific reasoning begins early on. We examine how children learn that "a lot" is "more than they need," and "a little" is "less than they want," and how they come to understand numbers and other symbols that quantify and manipulate different amounts of things.

Perhaps the most valuable lesson from our research is insight into the stages through which infants, young children, and older children learn to think and problem-solve. These stages redefine the learning experience and potential for children and adults of all ages. Thinking skills are the primary foundation of academic work. Nowadays, however, they are often a random by-product of education rather than a goal.

Sometimes educators and parents focus on memory-based learning rather than thinking-based learning. Children often reel off multiplication tables or math facts with great speed but little comprehension. If a child recites "two plus three is five" or runs through the alphabet, he feels his work is done. But what if the child doesn't really appreciate that five is a larger amount than two? To do this, he needs to be able to hold pictures in his mind of the relative quantities. Memory-based learning won't get children beyond the second grade. There's no harm in using memory plus thinking as long as it's not memory instead of thinking. As children develop in school, they must comprehend more than a fact in a passage. They must be able to think—to figure out, pull apart, and manipulate the ideas. The steps to develop this natural gift are formed right from the start and can be strengthened at any stage.

In this book we use the metaphor of a tree, the Learning Tree, to embody the three essential ingredients of learning: *Roots* represent the different ways children take in information and plan their actions (for example, how they decode what they hear, see, smell, or touch). The *trunk* of the tree represents thinking skills, the development of increasingly complex ways of thinking and, importantly, their application not only in academic subjects but also in such areas as friendships and family relationships. The *branches* represent the essential academic skills of reading, math, speaking, writing, and organizing.

The roots, always searching for nourishment, take in and process information. It is at this level that processing difficulties, such as hearing (auditory) or seeing (visual-spatial), need to be addressed. The trunk, the core of children's being, integrates and reformulates this information so that they can think. Thinking skills organize intellectual, emotional, and social functioning. The branches, with their showy flowers and fruit, represent the specific academic skill areas, where difficulties are more easily recognized. To let them blossom, the other parts of the tree must be strong and healthy. Other approaches often neglect this fact.

The idea of the Learning Tree is for all children—children with learning challenges can turn them into strengths; children with learning strengths can keep building on them. By identifying the building blocks that lead to following directions, reading, writing, doing math, and understanding science, history, and social studies—in essence, to all kinds of learning—we have found new methods for helping children with learning difficulties. Strengthening thinking and problem-solving can help any child, even one with the most severe learning disabilities, become a creative, reflective individual.

Our explanation starts with the earliest years because that is when the building blocks are formed. Throughout we show:

1. How each of the child's critical abilities and skills develops;
2. How the child's emotions not only mobilize his interest and motivation but also orchestrate learning;
3. How the child uses all senses and motor skills at each level of thinking;
4. How the child learns to apply reason and thought to all of life's situations.

For the most part, the book addresses parents. However, this information is as important for teachers as for parents, especially the last section.

It is probable that the child about whom you have specific questions is school-age. Our book, however, starts with very early learning. A child's developmental map for the early years may seem irrelevant to you. But do read these sections carefully. The steps that may need strengthening to improve your child's reading, math, or following of directions are ones that usually are built during these early years.

You can use this information in a couple of ways. One is merely to understand development. The other is to reflect on your own child's early behavior patterns. Once you understand those formative blocks, thinking back to the earlier years of your son or daughter may help you recognize some signs from that time and so help you identify the source of problems interfering with learning now. Even if nothing comes immediately to mind, one of these building blocks will most likely be the key to solving the current problem.

Traditionally, helping children with learning problems meant either improving their sensory systems, such as vision, or increasing practice on the particular problem, such as reading. All this was useful. But our emphasis is on how children learn to think. The developmental approach explained here integrates the sensory systems with a new understanding of what goes into thinking. Out of this union come solutions that are at the core of most school problems. Once established, a dynamic thinking process matures as the child matures because it incorporates all the fundamental skills. Hence the metaphor of a tree, whose roots bring in the nutrients and supply them to the trunk, which supports the branches. When they all work together, the tree thrives.

In Part One of the book, we introduce you to Sally and the difficulties she has with school and friends and show how the Learning

Tree approach helps such a child. Because testing is of such concern, even in the early grades, we then discuss its uses and misuses, including IQ testing. In Part Two, we introduce the role of play in learning and our method of using play and everyday interactions, which we call Floortime, to support a child's learning at every step. We then address how to strengthen the tree trunk—the thinking levels. These chapters on the levels of thinking, together with those in Part Three on the roots—on all the sensory systems— build the foundation for identifying the real reason behind why "Johnny can't read." Boxed questions in each chapter help parents identify whether more work is needed. Finally, in Part Four, we address the branches, the academic skills needed for success in school and in adult life. Here is where you will find specific solutions to particular problems, basically the three "Rs": struggles with reading and comprehension, with how to write an essay, and with math and nonverbal problems, plus "O" for organization. Wanting answers to your child's immediate difficulties, you may have the urge to start at the end, but without understanding the underlying issues first, you won't get to the cause of the problem. The solutions in Part Four require an understanding of basic thinking skills and of a child's sensory profile, which we help you identify in Part Three.

In addition, interspersed throughout the book, we have examples of how these thinking levels are embraced in a school curriculum. They come from the teachers at the Sidwell Friends Lower School, Washington, DC. We thank Dr. Richard Lodish, the associate head of school and head of the lower school, for providing these examples and writing these chapters. We thank the teachers for sharing the rich learning environment they have created.

Good, meaningful education should meet each child where he is. With the right developmental experiences, children will scale the educational ladder. Ultimately, we want education to prepare children for life, to help them become reflective thinkers, clear communicators, and organized problem-solvers in their families, work, and communities. To achieve this, we need to help them master enough of the basic learning skills so that their own motivation takes over and lets them enjoy and embrace the rich, complex world of ideas. If a child doesn't like to read, it's probably because reading is difficult for him. At six, he doesn't have a sense of how hard or easy it should be. He just knows that it's not fun, and he'd rather do something that's easier for him, something where he can achieve. We want children to achieve at reading and to enjoy it too.

PART ONE
THE LEARNING
TREE APPROACH

Marilyn Nolt

Sally's Story

In this chapter, we give you Sally's story, which shows our approach to learning problems and their causes. Later chapters will explain the concepts and cover specific problems and solutions in greater depth.

Nine-year-old Sally ambled along the sidewalk on her way home from school. She was lost in her thoughts as usual. They were not particularly happy thoughts. School had been tough today, like a lot of other days. In her mind she talked it over and over to herself.

If only the teacher didn't call on me to read, she thought. *Maybe it wouldn't be so bad. Everything is always awful after that. Especially after I make so many mistakes. I'm really dumb! I can't read fast. I can't follow her directions. Sometimes I can't do anything right.*

Sally was particularly hard on herself after a poor reading performance. She felt embarrassed in front of her classmates because of her struggles to read. Her confusion with following the teacher's instructions didn't help either. *It's so hard to know what the teacher wants me to do,* she thought to herself. *There are just too many steps. If I ask the teacher for help with the directions, the girls will really know*

3

I'm dumb. I wonder what they think of me? Maybe they laugh at me when I'm not around.

These thoughts easily triggered ones about the other girls in the class. *They probably don't like me very much. Sometimes they're nice; sometimes they're not. Do they like me? I can't tell. I just wish I could be their friend. Will they let me play at recess? I wish I weren't so scared to try. Maybe I'll never be able to talk to these girls,* she worried. Things churned away in her mind.

The cloud of gloom still hovered over Sally when she arrived home. Her mother knew immediately that it had been another unhappy school day. She was ready with a sympathetic ear, and Sally's disappointments tumbled out. She heard Sally's embarrassment with the reading exercise and her frustration with the directions; she listened to her describe her confusion about how some of the girls treated her: "Sometimes," Sally admitted to her mother, "I don't know if the girls are teasing me at recess to be friendly or if they're really trying to be mean. I don't know if I should talk to them or not. And at recess, it's so noisy."

Poor Sally! Her mom gave her a hug. It wasn't easy for Mom either—to see her little girl so sad. She didn't really know how to help, except to listen to Sally talk about her problems and feelings and to encourage her in the things she did well.

And Sally did have talents. She loved to draw and had become a very good artist. She was a natural navigator, helping her mother reach even hard-to-find destinations and then getting back. At home, she always had thoughtful opinions, making for lively dinner conversations between her and her brother. And, even with the distresses at school, she was good-natured.

However, her mother also knew that Sally had some difficulties. Her physical coordination was not very well developed, hence her poor performance in dance and sports. Her difficulties with body control and awareness, sometimes confusing the left and right sides of her body, confounded this. After a PE class made her feel clumsy, when she had trouble balancing on one leg or holding a position with her eyes closed, Sally would fret to herself almost as much as after a reading disaster.

There were several problems with Sally's reading. Any word of more than two syllables confused her. She stumbled when she got anxious. When the teacher asked her questions, such as, "What is the author getting at?" or "What's the theme here?" Sally's comprehension was poor. The teacher, hoping that more practice in class would help her improve, called on Sally frequently.

Sally's story is shared by many children: a learning problem, embarrassment at school, awkwardness with classmates, and a feeling of failure. In a situation such as Sally's, parents frequently consult with a reading specialist. But children who have trouble reading often have more fundamental problems—ones that don't necessarily seem related to difficulty with reading. These deeper problems can ripple through other academic areas as well as emotional and social areas. Without addressing them, the improvement gained from a specific remedial reading technique will usually prove limited.

All of this is to say that a specific learning problem that might pop up in school may be just the tip of the iceberg (but don't panic—think small iceberg). That is why the whole child needs to be appreciated and understood in order to overcome it. Given the uniqueness of each child and the host of basic building blocks that comprise the foundation of learning, anyone trying to put the pieces together and work out the appropriate solution for that child needs a systematic approach.

Hence the Learning Tree, which offers a step-by-step method. But before discussing how to sort it out, let's go into Sally's problems in a little more depth.

EXAMINING SALLY'S PROBLEMS

First off, let's look at her reading: Sally was missing one of the basics for learning to sound out new words (that is, read phonemically). For example, to connect a sound, such as "buh," to the visual image of the letter "b," you have to hear and visualize the difference between the letters in "buh" and "duh," "guh," or "huh." You must be able to hear this sound if it is an accented syllable or an unaccented one, and you must appreciate the rhythm of the word. Some children, and even adults, find these distinctions difficult to hear. If you have a "tin ear," which I confess I have, you will have a harder time learning to read.

Children with very good memories often skip over practicing this skill because they simply memorize the words whole. But even for these children, refining their ear and practicing to discriminate between different sounds can be worthwhile and important. What if your child wants to become a diplomat or maybe an opera singer who needs to speak several languages? Distinguishing between French "e"s with different accents can bedevil nonnative speakers, even those with good ears.

Sally's problem discriminating between sounds was only the beginning. It caused others: she couldn't hold in mind three- or four-step sound sequences (i.e., multisyllabic words). She found it difficult to sequence many sounds in a row because she couldn't hold onto the particular sounds well enough to remember the order. So she had two problems in terms of processing information: distinguishing between different sounds and then sequencing these sounds—often signs of a more fundamental concern, that of sequencing in general.

Sally was aware that she had a problem with sequencing, even though she couldn't articulate it. She knew that when her teacher gave her directions with many steps, she had a hard time holding them in mind and figuring out what came next. Whether it was directions about a writing assignment in class or a homework assignment, she became confused. Because Sally's mother helped to organize her homework, her teacher didn't realize the degree of her organizational problems. Of course, in class, her embarrassment from her reading mistakes only made these problems worse. To follow directions and organize her thoughts, she needed as much focus as she could muster. Anxiety caused her sequencing issues to get even worse.

One day in class she had to read a passage aloud from *Huckleberry Finn*, while someone else read one from *Tom Sawyer*. Everyone then had to write a one-page essay comparing the passages about the two boys. Even with some uncertainty in comprehending what she had read, she could see specific differences between Tom and Huck, who intrigued her, but after the trauma of reading, she felt too scattered to organize the thoughts needed to make the comparison. Instead she wrote only about Huck.

(An aside—Tom and Huck have kindly agreed to be frequent visitors to these pages and examples.)

So far, we have seen Sally's school difficulties expand from being unable to discriminate between sounds, to being unable to sequence these sounds, and finally to being unable to follow directions and organize her work. She also had a related problem in a different area of her life: she had as much trouble reading the subtle nuances in people's intentions as she did reading the words on a page. This led to her perplexity about whether the other girls liked her.

If your child has learning problems, she may also have struggles with friendships that are more exaggerated than those of other children. This is because the same problems that affect learning can affect relationships. In Sally's case, her difficulty in distinguishing the subtleties in sounds and words—called an auditory processing problem—that affected her schoolwork also affected her social skills, particularly in large groups like on the playground or at a party, where she had to process much verbal input quickly in a noisy setting.

Sally was a warm and friendly person and did have friends, in particular two close ones from her kindergarten days. But on the playground with the "cool kids," as she described them, it was more complicated. She couldn't tell when they were putting her down, when they were joking, or when they were being nice. She sometimes assumed that people didn't like her, only to discover later— through someone else—that so-and-so did like her. She could see that her other friends felt comfortable with these kids, but she knew that she felt nervous around them.

Although the connections between Sally's academic problems and social problems may not be obvious at first, it makes sense when you think about it. To figure out if someone's being mean-spirited or is just teasing requires a good ear. The slightest difference in tone of voice changes the message. Sally had a hard time with interpreting what she heard. Not surprisingly, she didn't have a very good sense of rhythm. Just as she had a "tin ear" for the rhythm of words and for people's intentions, she also had a "tin ear" for music, as evident in her frustrated efforts to play the piano.

SORTING OUT SALLY'S PROBLEMS

Sally's problem with reading is rather a complex picture. In my experience, this is pretty characteristic of children with learning disabilities. Their profiles are generally complex, with the child having relative strengths and relative weaknesses. Before we can help Sally—or any child with learning disabilities—we have to understand her strengths and weaknesses in all areas of her life because addressing the surface problem may help her only a little bit or may not help her at all. A child's problems with reading, math, speaking or writing, attention, or organization are often, as we mentioned, the tip of the iceberg.

So where do Sally's problems lie? In trying to uncover what is behind a learning problem and to figure out the solution, I like to start by looking at how a child functions in her daily life—emotionally, socially, and intellectually. By sizing up her general strengths and weaknesses, you can get a quick glimpse of the big picture. If there are real strengths here, you can use them to find strategies to solve the problems.

From Sally's story, we can see that she had strengths. On the emotional side, she had a lot of warmth and could talk about her feelings. On the social side, she had friends and close relationships with her family. On the intellectual side, she could be logical and creative. In supportive settings, she had no problems with being focused and attentive. She could engage in complex levels of thinking.

Let's separate out Sally's abilities and problems according to the three parts of our Learning Tree: the trunk, or level of thinking; the roots, or sensory systems; and the branches, or specific academic skills.

The Trunk

A child's thinking ability is what we refer to as the trunk of our Learning Tree. The three chapters in the next section provide a full explanation of the nine levels of thinking, but for now, let's just say that obviously the thinking of a two-year-old is not as sophisticated as that of a nine-year-old. As we age, we constantly build higher and higher levels of thinking. Sometimes we get stuck on a level or in times of stress lose some of our more sophisticated thinking abilities—this latter problem being more pronounced for children with learning difficulties.

By age nine, Sally's age, we expect children to have begun the highest level, to be reflective. For instance, a child might say, "Gee, it doesn't usually bother me, but I'm really upset about being picked last for softball today." Sally had the capacity to move toward reflective thinking. Remember that when she came home from school, she said to her mom, "I don't know if the girls at school are teasing me to be friendly or if they're really trying to be mean." This comment may seem as though she was just confused, but this is only part of the picture. She did not simply act on one or the other assumption and say, "They're all mean and they hate me," or, "Oh, they're all my friends, and they like me." These kinds of responses would imply an black-and-white, polarized way of looking at the world. Instead, she said, "It really confuses me," which indicates that she is self-aware.

So Sally had the fundamentals in place, but these basic abilities weren't as stable or as broad-ranging as we would like because when she got anxious and unsure of herself, her level of thinking fell. It could then become polarized, all-or-nothing. Though she was able to reflect on her relations with other girls, even when stressed about their liking her, she sometimes lost that reflective ability when she thought about her own intelligence. For instance, when Sally felt badly about her problem with reading, she would regress and say things such as, "I'm dumb because I can't read as fast as so-and-so" or "I'm dumb because I got a C on my exam." Her thinking abilities weren't as flexible and stable as they should be, but the fact that they were often present let us know that she had a lot of potential.

The Roots

Next, we need to look at the roots of the Learning Tree, the sensory systems. There, we saw that Sally had difficulty comprehending subtleties of sounds and sequencing them. Her sequencing problems extended to following directions. When she read, it was hard for her to connect the sounds to the letters. This made her a halting reader and slowed down the information that she could take in.

It also turned out that she was generally hypersensitive to loud sounds. Noisy situations, such as on the playground, could easily overload and confuse her and cause her thinking level to regress more readily. Together with her problems with motor planning and sense of her body in space (her poor performance in gym class), this could create a stressful playtime.

Fortunately, another root, her relatively strong visual-spatial capacities (she could easily help her mom navigate through town), helped her not get too lost or fragmented. When she got over-loaded, she could still hold on to a sense of who and where she was.

The Branches

Analyzing Sally's trunk and root systems gives us a way of under-standing her initial problem—her reading disorder—which is one of the branches, or specific academic skills. This is not the only branch with which she had difficulty. Her sequencing problems gave her dif-ficulty in speaking and writing as well as in following directions. Her organizational problems (another branch) had not been noticed be-cause her mother helped her organize her homework and studying, but they were significant. On the other hand, her good spatial sense meant that she had a good feel for math—she could picture quantity and space—and certain aspects of science. And her well-developed fine motor control made handwriting and drawing easy.

HELPING SALLY FROM THE GROUND UP

How does this picture of Sally translate into a comprehensive inter-vention program? To strengthen the branches (her schoolwork), we need to strengthen the root system and the tree trunk simultaneously.

1. Strengthen her reflective thinking skills. The first step is to help Sally develop her reflective thinking skills so that she won't regress to a lower level of thinking when she gets anxious. When she gets confused or anxious, we want her to say to herself, "When I get this feeling, I need to remember to pay more attention to my teacher and what she's saying. If I can listen the second time she gives the directions or raise my hand without worrying about feeling dumb, I can figure out what's going on." We want to help Sally recognize what happens to her when she criticizes herself with, "I'm dumb," and to use that feeling as a signal to pay more attention as well as to remember that she has wonderful strengths to draw on.

We want the same thing to happen when Sally is on the playground: when she's getting overloaded or unsure of herself, we want her to pay more attention to what the other kids are saying to figure out whether it deserves a laugh or, on the other hand, a competitive put-down (because sometimes you've got to protect yourself). Basically, we want to help Sally to be a reflective thinker more of the time. Then she can stay in the ballgame and even compensate for some of her planning and sequencing problems. For example, she can use her strong visual skills to diagram her essays with little boxes reminding her of what she wants to prove or to draw plans of the homework she has to get done.

2. Strengthen her auditory processing and sequencing. At the same time, we want to strengthen Sally's sensory system with a series of exercises to develop her auditory processing. We'll use a program of fun games to improve her basic skills in distinguishing sounds and connecting them to visual images. This will help considerably with her reading. We'll also work on her sequencing skills and her ability to follow verbal directions by initiating treasure hunt games in which she's motivated to follow increasingly complex directions. This will also help with her gross motor skills so that she becomes more confident in her body; learns her left from her right; and improves her balance, her coordination, and her dancing and athletic skills. We'll make heavy use of her visual-spatial strength—the fact that she can picture things very well—to strengthen all the other roots.

3. Diminish her sensory overreaction. Another aspect of strengthening the roots is to help Sally diminish her sensory overreactivity. She needs to develop strategies to take control of her environment and not get so overwhelmed. One of the problems with sensory overreactivity is the secondary anxiety you feel if you get overwhelmed by sound, touch, sight, or smells. Once you're anxious, you're even more hypersensitive. If Sally learns to go off for a short time to get a break from the noise, she will develop a sense of control and won't have that secondary anxiety. In fact, over time, her sensitivities will probably decrease because her secondary anxiety will decrease.

With the Learning Tree approach, we will not only help Sally with her immediate problem but will also build the foundation for stronger functioning on all levels. We will go into our methods for doing this in the chapters that follow. One area mentioned above that we do not explore further in this book is that of social relationships. This topic is covered in our book *Playground Politics*. We introduced it into Sally's story because it completes the whole developmental panorama and because it can be related to learning problems. Consequently, mastering the thinking skills in the Learning Tree can help build social skills.

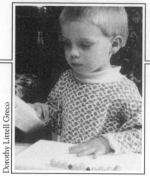

2

IQ Testing
Uses and Misuses

When you have a school-age child with learning problems, you will hear a lot about IQ and IQ testing. Understandably, parents worry about them. If a child has trouble reading, parents wonder whether this is a disability he can overcome and whether it means he lacks intelligence. These are very difficult questions for any parent to ponder.

Over the years, the educational system has relied on an IQ score to sum up a child's intelligence and to define whether a child might have some "cognitive deficits." A child who gets around 100 on his IQ is considered average, 110 is high average, 120 is getting into the superior range, and then 130 and above is in the very superior range. The child whose score is around 90 is in the low-average range, around 80 is the gray area of very low average to mild to severe cognitive deficits, and below that come different levels of "mental retardation." What does all this mean for a child with learning problems?

Let's look at what an IQ test is. Essentially, it is a series of standardized tests, some involving the visual system, some involving

14

language, some involving motor planning and sequencing, and some involving the speed of the motor system. Yes, all the cognitive capacities of our Learning Tree are tapped by an IQ test. But the question becomes, are the tasks included in the IQ test necessarily the best assessment of each of these aspects? The answer is a definitive "No." If we want to assess a child's motor skills and spatial problem-solving, we should offer ten or fifteen tasks in that area, not just one or two. So, the test doesn't tell you anything more than how the child does on that particular exercise or those particular skill-based items. It can be useful to have that information, and you can sometimes make inferences, perhaps get hints of strengths or weaknesses. For instance, if the child does well on the vocabulary and picture sequencing tests but not very well on the object assembly test, he probably has a good memory but isn't very good at spatial problem-solving.

Put succinctly, an IQ test is not a complete profile, and its total score does not render a verdict.

What else should be considered in looking at a child's level of intelligence? In terms of our Learning Tree trunk, we need to look at the level of the child's thinking skills and the social and emotional capacities that go along with and support them. This provides us with a framework for thinking about intelligence in a broader way. Rather than an IQ score on a single test, we can evaluate a child's level of intelligence by looking at his cognitive, sensory, and emotional development across a full range of human endeavors, academic and nonacademic. To figure out where a child needs help, we are much better off analyzing each of the capacities of the root and trunk system and then looking at how the child performs in the various branches.

Mental functioning is a dynamic, growing process. Just because a child is behind now does not mean he'll be behind next year or five years from now. We have to look at the child's learning curve over time. If a child has not had opportunities to master a specific think-ing skill, there's no reason for him to be competent in that area. We need to provide him with a rich environment that develops that skill and to watch what happens to his learning curve. Interestingly, this view is quite similar to that of Alfred Binet, whose name is so closely entwined with IQ testing. He felt that thinking abilities were not set, that remedial work could improve weak areas. And he was clearly opposed to those who looked at IQ as a determining score:

> Some recent philosophers seem to have given their moral support to these deplorable verdicts by affirming that an individual's intel-ligence is a fixed quantity, a quantity that cannot be increased. We must protest and react against this brutal pessimism; we must try to demonstrate that it is founded on nothing. (*Les ideés modernes sur les enfants*, 1909)

In general, I refuse to make a diagnosis of a cognitive deficit or mental retardation until I have had a chance to orchestrate as ideal a program as possible to mobilize the child's learning, growth, and development for at least two years. As long as the learning curve slopes upward during those two years, there should not be talk of a cognitive deficit, other than in a temporary sense, and certainly not mental retardation, which implies something permanent.

If your child has developed solid thinking skills and strengthened all the sensory systems—a strong tree trunk with a good root system—he is ready for school learning. The actual effort involved in master-ing academic subjects should go smoothly. If your child still needs to work on some of the sensory skills, that's all right. Whenever he comes to a hurdle in learning to read, do math, write, communicate orally, or be organized, go back to the tree trunk and root system and see if there's more fundamental work to be done. If so, go back to the exercises that we will describe in this book and strengthen that sense.

PART TWO
THE TRUNK

Play and Learning
Floortime

Playtime is a child's world. A time of imagination and make-believe, of games and hanging out, of spontaneous curiosity. Playtime evokes images of dolls, dress up, hide-and-seek, and hopscotch. Scenes of five-year-olds romping about with other five-year-olds, two-year-olds in a sandbox, ten-year-olds playing Marco Polo. On the surface, play is simply fun, an exciting part of life.

For a glimpse of these moments, think back to the adventures of that quintessential pack of kids, the *Little Rascals*. But then look again. Whether flying kites, organizing follies, escaping from pirates, or starting a detective agency, this gang took control, made decisions, and scraped through. Presto! Out of casual play, a child's intellect matures and grows.

Recently play has garnered appreciation as something almost magical in quality given its seemingly humble beginnings. Imagination, self-control, and planning are but a few of the qualities associated with free, creative play. This assessment rings true with dramatic escapades in the backyard as well as turning over rocks and eyeing the busy world beneath. Left to their own devices—needing little to no assistance from the toys, lessons, computer games, and TV of nowadays—children will let their imaginations flourish.

Parents enter this world of their children too—running around, tossing a ball, swinging—just having fun. Playtime is an opportunity for children and parents to connect, share, and bond. These times are special enough as is, but there's more to them: play, as we will see, can have an added dimension and an enhanced agenda, which are especially beneficial for children with learning disabilities, but also for all children.

With little children, this particular kind of play begins with getting down on the floor and so we named it Floortime, but it works just as well standing or sitting. The first goal of Floortime is to make it easier for adults to be welcomed into a child's world. The second goal is the goal of this book: to support a child's thinking. This means paying attention to your child in a very specific way during pretend play or, equally important, during everyday spontaneous exchanges.

All children gain from this extra boost. But children with learning difficulties gain—and *need* it—the most.

What Exactly Is Floortime?

Well, as the name suggests, you get down on the floor and play, but it is a special kind of play. In Floortime, the play excites your child's interests, draws her to connect to you, and challenges her to be creative, curious, and spontaneous—all of which move her forward intellectually and emotionally. Floortime is a way of being together wherever you are. (As your children get older, Floortime essentially morphs into hang-out time.) For a child of any age, you do three things: 1) follow your child's lead—in other words, don't take over the pretend play or game; 2) challenge her to be creative and spontaneous; and 3) expand the action and interaction to include all or most of her senses and motor skills as well as different emotions. As you do all this, while staying within her focus, you are helping her practice basic thinking skills. To master these skills and improve learning problems require using all these senses, emotions, and motor skills, as this book will explain.

Sometimes it's easy to forget that the play is the child's to direct, not yours. She has the starring role. You are merely a fun—and nonintrusive—supporting actor. For most parents, this is a role cast against type, and one for which most of us would not win an Oscar. It can definitely require some practice, especially for parents who may not be good followers. It is hard to let go of being the boss, but that is what you need to do. However, even though you are not the boss, you can be a follower who adds to the drama. You are not a passive partner. While your child directs the drama, you can subtly help the drama get richer.

Learning the Floortime process has some similarities to learning a foreign language. At first you have to think, plan, and make an effort to communicate effectively. But once you learn to think within the new context and become comfortable with the new patterns, the process eventually becomes natural and is its own reward.

Floortime with Bradley

Five-year-old Bradley is pushing a bulldozer along the floor, the front scoop shoving aside all obstacles that block its path. Matchbox cars, G. I. Joes, and Transformers lie in its wake. The clatter of power and the roar of the engine (Bradley's vocal additions) fill the room. Mom walks in, says hi, and is completely ignored. Whether Bradley is too wrapped up in his bulldozer even to hear Mom or just doesn't want to take the time to respond isn't clear and doesn't matter to Mom. She sees an opportunity to have some fun too.

With a giggle, she carefully puts her foot into the bulldozer's path and announces, with shoulders squared, a deep voice, and a firmly set mouth, "Ho, Ho, Mr. Mighty Bulldozer. I'm a big heap of trash. I bet you can't push me aside." Somewhat surprised but up for the task, Bradley tries to figure out what to do. Can the bulldozer move the foot/trash? Or does it have to go over or around it? It's worth a try, so, with his own determined look, he directs the bulldozer to push against his mom's shoe, and sure enough Mom is no match for the mighty bulldozer. Her foot gives way, and Bradley, with a new gleam in his eye, lets his bulldozer exclaim, "I am mighty," and continues to cut a swath through all the toys.

Now down on the floor, Mom picks up G. I. Joe in one hand and a Transformer in the other. As she makes them both "run" toward the bulldozer, they "tell" Bradley, "We are so fast, we will run and jump onto Mr. Mighty Bulldozer." The bulldozer says, "You can't catch me," and Bradley makes it swerve. Heavy "Ohs!" and "Ahs!" escape from the two pursuers. No matter how hard they try, they just can't catch up to the bulldozer. Finally they announce, "We give up!" and ask, because they tried so hard, "Can we have a ride just for fun?" Bradley mulls this over for a few seconds and says, "Okay, just a short one." Mom hands G. I. Joe and the Transformer to Bradley to put them on the bulldozer. She wonders if they need help to stay on or if they can balance by themselves. Bradley tells her not to help. He can balance both on top of the bulldozer. "Mr. Mighty Bulldozer will go slower," he says. They stay on, but when the bulldozer races a little faster—crash! Off they go. Mom says, "Wow! They're tough. They didn't get hurt, but they sure do look tired. Maybe they need to sit for awhile." Bradley agrees, and she says that she will come back later when they have rested. Bradley thinks that's okay.

So how did Floortime with Mom help develop Bradley's thinking? Mom did many wonderful things with Bradley: She followed his lead, she challenged him to be creative, and she expanded their interactions. She enriched Bradley's play in ways that encourage the first six levels of thinking that we will describe in detail in the next chapter.

First, Mom got Bradley's attention and interest, which is the first level of thinking—taking an interest in the world. She broadened his interest in a playful way to include her and her "trash pile." At the same time, she enticed him to play with her and thoroughly enjoy it. Engaging with other people is the second level. While this was going on, Mom and Bradley exchanged not only words but also many animated facial expressions, arm gestures, and the like, and their voices took on many different intonations. In other words, there was a vivid, nonverbal dialogue with gestures going on as well as rich, expressive vocalizations—what we call interaction (two-way communication) or the third level. Mom engaged Bradley in problem-solving—the fourth level. Bradley had to figure out how to get through or around the trash pile and how to keep G. I. Joe and the Transformer balanced on the bulldozer.

Mom also gave Bradley opportunity to use ideas more meaningfully and creatively, which is the fifth level. Rather than just zooming around and banging into things (as Bradley was doing on his own), Mr. Mighty Bulldozer busted through the trash pile, ran away from two indomitable pursuers, and frustrated their efforts to catch him. A drama unfolded between Bradley and Mom as they connected new ideas together. Connecting ideas logically is the sixth level.

The pretend play with Mom drew on all of Bradley's senses and processing areas (i.e., the roots)—auditory, language, visual-spatial thinking, sensory modulation, and motor planning and sequencing—strengthening them simultaneously. (These are described and treated separately in Part Three.)

The fact that Mom did all this—have fun, follow Bradley's lead, and entice Bradley to have fun with her—while challenging him to expand his interactions and drama is a testimony to Mom's skill and natural ability. I have only one suggestion for Mom. At the end, she took over the drama. Did you catch it? At the end, she suggests that

G. I. Joe and the Transformer rest, but a better alternative would be for her to ask, "Bradley, what do you think they want to do, after such an exciting chase?" That way, Bradley would continue to be the director and scriptwriter, that is, the boss of the drama. Bradley might have said that they were tired, exhausted, angry at losing, or that they wanted to do more. If he wanted to continue and Mom had to leave to get his older sister at school, she could explain the situation and ask him if there is something else G. I. Joe, the Transformer, and the bulldozer could do for a short time while she was away, giving him the opportunity to decide the plans for his toys.

However, it isn't necessary to be "perfect." This mom did a really good job. There will be endless chances for strengthening the elements of learning through play and all the everyday activities and interactions of family life as long as parents become aware of these opportunities.

The Importance of Challenges

Remember that Floortime is merely a tool, a process, enabling you to enter your child's world and help her strengthen her levels of thinking. Again, the three steps are 1) follow; 2) challenge; and 3) expand.

Here, let me emphasize the second step, to challenge. Often, I see Floortime described as "following the child's lead during playtime." This basic element, although necessary, does not define Floortime. Once a child is at the problem-solving level, she needs gentle challenges in her interactions with you to continue reaching new levels of thinking. You can ask her questions about what you should do, act confused about what your toy should do, sometimes play dumb—all to encourage your child to come up with her own ideas. This encourages thinking in any child, but for an eight-year-old who can't quite make connections between ideas, it is critical.

Think of it this way: Floortime as a Socratic method for children—asking questions (including nonverbal ones through gesturing) to get children thinking. It isn't necessary to take the analogy too far. The questioning part, getting the child to think on her own, make up her own mind, is enough. It lets the child be the boss, figure out problems, and take responsibility for her actions.

You can have these Socrates Moments in spontaneous interactions as well as in Floortime sessions. All the everyday interactions in a family can spur learning throughout a child's waking hours—eating dinner, getting ready for school, helping with chores, walking the dog, going shopping, or discussing what TV show to watch—these are chances for a child's ideas to flourish. Riding in the car is a big opportunity for casual chitchat and a lot of questions. You can ask your children why they want to do something; you can ask if they want treat A or B; you can give them a choice of activities so that they have to explain their preferences. It isn't a drill or cross-examination. In some ways, the exchange is similar to when we meet someone we like and want as a friend: being interested and engaged, asking questions. With a new friend, we want to learn about the person and develop a rapport, just as with our fascinating, constantly developing children. With our children, there is a dual benefit. We are also giving them opportunities for thinking and expanding their ideas.

These everyday exchanges can be an opportunity to listen attentively to what your child has to say (follow), to ask questions to get a better understanding (challenge), and to support your child's new ideas that come from your questions (expand).

Floortime on the Monkey Bars

In the earlier example with Bradley, Mom happened upon an already developing drama and entered it. Just as easily, Bradley and Mom could be at the playground. Bradley, on the top rung of the ladder at the end of the monkey bars, reaches up to grab a bar, hangs from it for a second, and with Mom's help, gets his feet back onto the ladder. Whenever they go to the playground, this is what Bradley likes to do, over and over. Even though Bradley is well co-ordinated and strong for his age, he goes no further. One day Mom tries to help him to do something new.

"Bradley, you do a great job of climbing and hanging from that bar," Mom says as he rests his feet on the ladder rung. "The next time, do you want to try to get to the second bar?"

"Nope," he answers, "I like this."

"Okay, Sweetie, but I have a big favor to ask you. Will you help me hang from the bar? I haven't done it for a long, long time, and I don't think I can do it by myself. If you helped me, it would make a big difference."

Bradley pauses. He likes helping his mom, especially if it is something he can do. "Yes," he says, feeling in charge, "I'll help."

Bradley climbs down, and Mom carefully climbs up the three rungs. "Oh, now what do I do," asks Mom.

"Put one hand on the bar and then the other hand," Bradley tells her. She does so gingerly. "Mommy, hold on tight and push off the ladder." She suddenly hangs down from the bar. "That's good."

"Well," shouts Mom, "you give really good directions. I want to try to get to the next bar. I'm not sure how to. What do you think? Can you help me?"

"Okay, I'll hold your legs and push them."

"What do I do with my hands?" she asks him.

"The same as before, one hand and then the other."

"OK, just hold me tightly, please." Putting her hands on the next bar and swinging, she exclaims, "Wow, I made it. Now I want to go back. Do you think holding my legs again will help me?"

"Yup," and Bradley does.

Mom puts her feet back on the ladder and asks, "What did you do that helped me so much?"

"Oh, I just pushed a little when I held your legs."

"Well, it worked. Great job. That was fun. Do you want to go back up the ladder?"

"My turn," says Bradley. He scampers back up and gets into his usual position to reach for the first bar. He pushes off and hangs down.

Mom asks, "If I hold onto your legs tightly like you did for me, do you want to try getting to the next bar? I'll be careful like you were with me. What do you think?"

Emboldened, Bradley says, "Yes, help me." And with Mom holding him, he reaches for the next bar, swings, then goes back to the first bar and onto the ladder. After this big breakthrough, every time they went to the playground, Bradley worked on the swinging rhythm to go farther and farther across the bars, at first with Mom's help and then on his own.

During this playtime, things were a little different. At first, Mom and Bradley were just having fun at the playground. The problem was that Bradley, a little scared and cautious, was simply repeating the same moves. Mom had to figure out how to challenge him (without taking over) so that his coordination and motor sequencing could keep growing. In this case, Mom couldn't pretend to be a trash pile to create a problem. Instead, she created a problem for herself; asked for Bradley's help to solve it, thus letting him be in charge; and took the opening to demonstrate the next movement. Once she had shown him, she gave him the choice to copy her. If Bradley had taken the initiative on his own, Mom would have merely been an appreciative playmate, doing what we all often do: asking our child if she can yell like Tarzan as she swings from bar to bar, or if she thinks monkeys might go across differently. The fun and imagination come naturally.

Some children may not agree to take risks at the first chance, but if given support and allowed to make the choice themselves, they eventually will. The same principles—follow, challenge, and expand—still hold.

The next two chapters describe the levels of thinking that children progress through to become insightful and thoughtful adults. Anywhere along the way, children can hit obstacles to advancing to the next level of thinking and may need some help. Floortime is a tool to overcome these obstacles.

Marilyn Nolt

4

Building Basic Thinking

Sally's story (related in Chapter 1) is fairly typical: learning problems, friendship anxieties, concerns about school. With our developmental approach, we can look beneath these problems to see what level of thinking a child has reached as well as how solid the foundation is. Most important, as with Sally, we can figure out what will establish the foundation and help a child overcome the problems by achieving higher levels of thinking.

Consider a child's advancing to a new level of thinking as analogous to what he experiences in maturing physically. One day a baby turns over—a new milestone. At first it may be only on one side and front to back. Soon it's both sides and both directions. At first it may be a bit of struggle, but shortly the motion becomes fluid, with the baby able to hold something in his hand while gracefully turning. The first awkward turn has expanded into one of grace, ease, and complexity, readying the baby for the next milestone of sitting up. And then on to stabilizing on all fours, crawling, pulling up, and then walking, with the execution of each milestone becoming more assured and more complex before the next one occurs.

Babies make the initial leap to the new level, and then they practice it in every way possible. They use the more advanced ability to explore their surroundings anew, and they bring along the old skills—touching, poking, grabbing, picking up, mouthing—into the new experiences. They seek, strive, and practice, not only the new skill but also the old ones in a different context. For instance, at some point, a baby can sit on the floor and push a ball to Dad. Once he learns to stand, he can, after awhile, push it with his foot. He has the same goal of making a ball roll, but it becomes a completely new experience that, with ever-improving coordination and balance, keeps development moving forward.

Exactly the same thing happens with learning to think. As a child's nervous system and the sensory systems develop, he can reach new milestones in thinking. With each new milestone, he experiences the same world around him but in new ways. A two-year-old simply enjoys the wonderment of a bird flying. A four-year-old, looking at the same bird, will wonder how it flies. He has reached a higher level of thinking, and each time he does so, he reorganizes and reexperiences what the senses bring. It's this reorganization that lets his thinking grow and makes his world bigger, richer, and more complex.

Making that level of thought—the new milestone—as strong as possible means a child needs to experiment with applying it to everything around him, both the old and the new. This includes how he thinks about what he sees, hears, plans, does, feels, and learns in school and everyplace else. As he applies his new thinking skill to familiar experiences and expands on them, his understanding deepens, and he solves more and more complex problems. His thinking capacities mature.

With proper care, the trunk of a child's Learning Tree grows to incorporate the nine milestones or levels of thinking that are essential for mature intellectual development. In this chapter and the next, we describe the nine levels of thinking, each more complex than the prior one. Those addressed in this chapter are the early ones: the ability to attend, to engage, to interact, to solve problems and sequence, to use ideas creatively and meaningfully, and to think logically. The description of the levels first presents the general concepts at the age-appropriate level so as to lay out the pathway clearly. Although there is some extension of these concepts to older children included, a set of questions at the end of each of the levels makes it easier for you to reflect on your older child's mastery of them. As you will see, the first couple of answers to the questions indicate a child who still needs to practice that level; the next answers indicate a child with a deeper capacity. This information helps you to determine whether your child has reached a certain level. Reaching the level is the first of three dimensions to mastering the level. The other two are developing a broad range on this level and maintaining its stability. Just picture your child 1) climbing up to and 2) standing on a broad, 3) stable platform.

We explore the breadth and range of the level when we discuss the development of specific senses (the roots). Answering the questions in the roots section about how well your child has integrated the senses at various levels can sometimes reveal uneven skills at a level or throughout the levels. For instance, at a particular level of thinking that seems generally strong, you may realize that the visual-spatial area is strong but that the auditory processing is weaker. This often translates into a child's being stronger in math and weaker in reading comprehension or the social sciences.

The third dimension relates to the stability of the level, that is, whether your child maintains the thinking level even under strong emotions, say, anxiety, anger, or excitement. We delve into this dimension in the conclusion to this section on the roots.

LEVEL ONE: ATTENTION

The earliest level of thinking starts to develop at birth. The examples that follow describe the baby and child as he first encounters the milestone. Your child is probably older than those in the examples, but they are meant to show just where the thinking levels start. The skills are needed at every age.

Some of the descriptions might bring to mind your own child at a younger age. You might even recognize some aspect of thinking with which your child had trouble. This could help pinpoint what needs work.

When a newborn opened his eyes and took in a whole new world, one of his first impressions was you, Mom and Dad, leaning over him in total wonderment at his existence. He smelled you, felt your touch, heard your voice, and saw something that over time more distinctly became your face. Your gentle sounds, touch, and facial expressions drew him to you and gave him pleasure. It is this emotion that you stirred up in him, this pleasure that he felt, that kept bringing him back to you, that made him want to pay attention. He used every sense to take you in and discover you because the most intriguing thing in his world is another person. The more sights and sounds, smells and touch, and movement patterns and different emotions your child encountered, the stronger his ability to pay attention became, but for some time you remained the most fascinating object in his universe.

Whether it's a nine-year-old raptly listening to his teacher explain how and why the moon goes around the Earth or a one-month-old hearing Mommy's or Daddy's sounds and watching their mouths move, paying attention is the first step in thinking. The child is involved with another person and ready to engage. Without it, he could be lost in his own inner world.

Level One: Attention

1a. Can your child focus and calmly perform routine tasks at home or at school in an age-appropriate manner when doing something he wants to do (for example, play a game of checkers with you)? My child is . . .

1. Unable to focus and perform routine tasks
2. Rarely able to focus and perform routine tasks
3. Sometimes able to focus and perform routine tasks
4. Usually able to focus and perform routine tasks

1b. Can your child focus and calmly perform routine tasks at home or at school in an age-appropriate manner when doing something that someone else wants him to do? My child is . . .

1. Unable to focus and perform routine tasks
2. Rarely able to focus and perform routine tasks
3. Sometimes able to focus and perform routine tasks
4. Usually able to focus and perform routine tasks

1c. Is your child able to control his impulses, fears, and anxieties and calm down with a little bit of support? My child is . . .

1. Unable to self-regulate
2. Rarely able to self-regulate, and then only if his feelings are not very intense
3. Sometimes able to self-regulate, even with strong feelings
4. Usually able to self-regulate, even under stress

LEVEL TWO: ENGAGING WITH THE WORLD

By two months, your child became ready to engage with you. Engagement, where one of you smiles and the other responds, or he coos and you coo back in a rhythmical, vocal interaction, created a growing bond that you two built on throughout the next years, both emotionally and intellectually. It was the start of a close relationship, of giving and receiving pleasure. Engagement in relationships is the way we learn that there is a world outside ourselves. It's the way we learn about emotions and social interaction. A sustained relationship with you allows trust, security, and intimacy to build. It is the fabric that keeps us all striving to fulfill and be fulfilled emotionally.

What does engagement mean for an older child, a seven-year-old? If he is engaged with and emotionally connected to his teacher, he will want to connect his ideas to hers when she asks him, "Who was George Washington?" even if he struggles to answer. The positive relationship he has formed with her will make him strive. In fact, his very capacity to have an opinion about people in history (or day-to-day life) depends on his having been part of a relationship in which he learns about other people's feelings. It is the same for the four-month-old whose big, wide-eyed smile reveals his happiness at seeing Dad. This gesture, a special smile for Dad, differentiating his emotions and engaging Dad, is a vital ingredient of thinking, even though he is not yet thinking with words.

Jonah

Eleven-month-old Jonah sits in his mother's lap, exploring her ear, looking at it, yanking on it a little bit, making gurgling sounds of fascination. Mother imitates his sounds with variations in tone and expression that suggest appreciation of and admiration for her toddler's curiosity. She lowers her head to make it easier for Jonah to look in her ear and gently touches one of his ears to show him the similarity. He puts his hand on hers and his own ear, and after exploring his ear together with her, she shows him her other ear, all the while making soft noises that respond to his and making eye contact, eyebrows raised and a look of pleasant surprise on her face as they discover the ear's firm and soft textures.

Mother follows Jonah's lead and constantly keeps a visual, vocal, and gestural connection to him. She is a good Floortimer (or, at this level, more precisely a "Laptimer") and keeps her son involved. Through many such games, the two can explore ears and noses, knees and elbows, and feet and hands together. In the play, Jonah uses many senses and motor skills. Through her enthusiastic interactions, Mom engages Jonah's curiosity about the world, which bolsters his sense of discovery and adventure.

Even with a baby, you can recognize whether he is engaged: "Is my baby interested in playing with me? Is he listening and vocalizing (or speaking, if just a little older)? Is he moving toward me, touching me, smelling (or even tasting) me? Are we in sync?" These senses, which we will see are the roots of learning, bring in the information out of which ideas can form.

You don't want to overwhelm yourself or your child by working too hard to get him stimulated and engaged. At the beginning, your most important task with a child of any age is to have fun and follow your child's lead. Getting into a rhythm will help the rest to occur. To do this may take some adjustment. The more sedentary among us might not move enough to engage a quiet baby. The Energizer-bunny types might not let a child's ideas develop enough and may need to slow down. Just think about your style, your child's style, and what you need to do to be engaging. We all can make changes if we are aware of what is needed.

Engaging at Every Age

Because the tree trunk expands very rapidly at the early ages, your child will soon be thinking at the next level. But remember, regardless of your child's age, whenever you play or chat, you need to make sure that your child is attentive and engaged with you before you get into more sophisticated interactions. As you sit on the floor, at the kitchen table, or in the car, the first question to ask yourself is: "Do I have my child's attention? Is he engaged with me?"

Here are a couple of examples for older kids. On a vacation day, when her friends are busy, a four-year-old little girl has been playing on her own all day. At this point she is letting her pony gallop around. Mom picks up another pony, exclaims how pretty the pony is, interjects an enthusiastic, "Nice pony," and asks if her pony can gallop alongside. Rather than changing the story or the subject, she becomes part of the play scenario, so her daughter can keep playing with the pony and let Mom enter the drama.

If a father is trying to play with his eight-year-old son, who'd rather mope and daydream all day, he can ask himself, "What's really going to draw him to me? A friend at school, a pet animal, a sports event?" Picking the most likely and starting a conversation about it can draw the child in. If it doesn't work this time, he can wait awhile and try another subject later, maybe changing the opening and approach.

You lose the game if you nag or start with a subject children are not interested in. Tap into their positive interests. That's where their emotions are. Emotions are the juice that gets everything connected and running. This is true for each of the levels of thinking. It may be easiest to notice the impact of using emotions at the early levels because a child's interests are easier to predict then. But emotions and the relationships that result from them keep us connected to the world at all ages, and it is through them that we continue to bring in more information and build higher levels of thinking.

Level Two: Engagement

2a. When your child is upset, overwhelmed, or in any type of discomfort, he typically . . .

1. Withdraws
2. Looks to someone for comfort, but is superficial and needy
3. Looks to someone, but if very overwhelmed sometimes shuts down and withdraws
4. Looks to someone close to her for comfort

2b. Or when your child is upset, overwhelmed, or in any type of discomfort, he typically . . .

1. Gets overly active and disorganized
2. Indiscriminately seeks comfort very quickly with whoever is around
3. Looks to the primary caregiver, but if very overwhelmed becomes active and indiscriminate, seeking closeness with anyone
4. Looks to the primary caregiver or very familiar person

2c. When you interact with your child, he is typically . . .

1. Uninvolved and/or cold and aloof
2. More involved when he wants something
3. Warm and caring some of the time
4. Warm and caring

LEVEL THREE:
INTERACTION AND COMMUNICATION

Children's thinking develops very quickly. After just four months or so, they are ready to add another level, that of interaction, which now involves *how* a child interacts—not just the fact that he is interacting. He has already done the latter by paying attention and engaging. Now a child reads signals and reacts to them.

Interaction means that conversation, whether verbal or nonverbal, is a continuous flow, a circle of communication. You or your child opens the circle with a sound or gesture (or obviously a comment/question with an older child), and the other closes it by responding directly to the effort. It's always two-way rather than you or the child simply saying something. During play or spontaneous interactions, you can tell whether you are opening and closing circles of communication with gestures and/or with words (ideally both, if the child is verbal) and stringing together many circles, opening and closing one after the other.

Nonverbal Communication

For a little child who is not yet verbal, the interactions will consist of many gestures in a row. For instance, the child has a ball, and Dad puts his hand out asking him for it; he puts it in Dad's hand. Dad offers it back to him, and he takes it. Two circles—in each Dad opens and he closes, back and forth, in a continuous flow. Perhaps after a few similar rounds, Dad varies the exchange by turning his palm over so the child can't see the ball. He wonders where it went. Dad then shows it to him again, and he takes it (longer circle). It's the same thing when eight-month-old Billy reaches out for a rattle. Mom holds it up a tiny bit higher, and Billy stretches farther to take it from Mom's hand. Mom lets Billy grab it.

Circles of communication—opening and closing, back and forth, flowing—teach children how to be purposeful or logical, how to make things happen in the world. It's the beginning of understanding cause and effect, the realization that "If I reach out, I can grab the rattle." As with the first two milestones, the basis of the conversation is an emotional connectedness that makes the circles go 'round.

Verbal Communication

For older children, these circles of communication become a real conversation. Six-year-old Monica opens a circle when she raises her hand in class, and her teacher says, "Monica, what do you want?" When Monica responds, "I want to tell the class what I did yesterday," she is closing the circle. It's a simple circle: she raises her hand, the teacher calls on her, and she gets to speak. But it's such basic communications that lead to elaborate conversations and higher levels of thinking.

A really good, flowing conversation starts with something your child is already interested in (just as with getting his attention). It could be dinosaurs or what he wants for a birthday present; it could be the new puppy or the pony rides at the fair. It could be why you are being unfair or why school is terrible! Go where the interest, experience, and emotional involvement are, and you'll see how long a conversation can keep going—the longer, the better. When you're having a long conversation with gestures and words, whether on the floor or at the dinner table or in the car or walking in the park, your child is learning to sequence many ideas in a row and to do so in a meaningful, responsive way.

Samantha

Five-year-old Samantha is talking with her dad about the bunny rabbit in the pet store that they plan to bring home. Dad asks her what she wants to name the bunny. "Oh, I don't know," she says. "Maybe I'll name her Floppy or maybe Fluffy."

"That's a tough choice. Why do you think Floppy is a good name?"

"Well, her ears flop down."

"Oh, right, she's a mini-lop. Her ears do flop down. That's a good reason. What about Fluffy?"

"Well," explains Samantha, "She is fluffy."

"Yes," says Dad, "that's true. So how are you going to decide?"

"I don't know," admits Samantha.

"Do you think you'll decide before you bring her home?" continues Dad.

"Well, maybe." And on and on.

Samantha, totally enthralled, could have talked about the bunny all day, so Dad had an easy time with a long, emotionally meaningful conversation. But not without Samantha first having participated in long, gestural exchanges as a one- and two-year-old. Of course, conversations don't always come as easily. The stereotype is a little boy, we'll call him Billy, who comes home from school. When he walks in, Mom asks, "How are you?"

"Fine."

"How was school?"

"Okay."

"What did you do today?"

"Nothing." And he takes off to his room. Although Billy answered her questions, this is not a continuous flow; it's a brick wall. (Of course, this is all relative. If Billy had never spoken and suddenly spoke these words, it would be a moment to cheer, a beginning to build on.) To get a real chat going, Mom needs to figure out what her son is most interested in and use that to open up the verbal spigot. It is important to keep trying. A child who finds it difficult to participate in a conversation needs practice. Weakness in this area is implicated in attention problems and other learning difficulties.

Counterbalancing

Sometimes with older children you find yourself at the proverbial "bringing the horse to water but can't make him drink" stage. You just can't get a flow going, as with Billy. A trick we call "counter-balancing" can help you lure your child.

Counterbalancing means that you—the parent, teacher, or caretaker—try to balance out the child's natural tendencies or a particular mood of the moment. For example, if the child is passive and uninvolved, you try to create some enthusiasm. For a child who is lying on the floor staring blankly while sucking his thumb, you add a little energy to stimulate his interaction with you. If the child is upset, you don't fuel the emotional fire by also being upset; you offer extra soothing and concern. If he squirms and squeals and runs about wildly, you impart some calm to get his attention.

The way in which children interact with their families becomes the way in which they interact with the world. If a child is constantly overwhelmed, he'll start feeling overwhelmed in many different settings and may tune out entirely. But if you help him to change that pattern and modulate his feelings, then he can go to a corner of the classroom and calm down when the noise gets to him, or ask to go to the nurse's office for a bit. He'll find some strategy to get back into a calm state because he's experienced what that state feels like and wants to re-create it for himself.

What should Mom do to get Billy involved? Clearly, given his responses, he isn't interested in her opening topics: his well-being, school, or his activities. She knows her son best. She needs to hone in on his interests, not what she wants to find out. Whether it's about a soccer game, doing something special with his dad, or making plans to visit a particular friend—after the initial "Hi," she needs to offer something that will perk up his ears. The conversation will follow.

Level Three:
Interaction and Communicating

3a. **When you are interacting with your child using gestures (for example, a smile or a funny face), he . . .**

1. Doesn't usually respond or interact very much
2. Only responds if you keep repeating the gesture or facial expression
3. Seems to get confused and interrupts the interaction
4. Responds when he understands the emotional gesture or expression, but this understanding is limited to only certain emotions
5. Responds and clearly understands a wide range of emotional expressions

3b. **When you are interacting with your child, he . . .**

1. Doesn't initiate emotional gestures and expressions on his own
2. Uses gestures and facial expressions if he is very excited about something
3. Initiates gestures within a certain range of emotions only
4. Feels comfortable initiating a wide range of emotional gestures and expressions

3c. **When you and your child are interacting or playing, your child . . .**

1. Cannot sustain a conversation
2. Can only sustain a brief conversation (20–30 seconds)
3. Sometimes can sustain a long conversation (5–10 minutes of gesturing and talking with you)
4. Most of the time can sustain a long conversation

LEVEL FOUR: SHARED PROBLEM-SOLVING

By the age of about eleven months, when a child has a good sense of two-way communication, his thinking will move to the fourth level, what we call shared social problem-solving. Now, with animated gestures and sounds, he can signal what he wants. When he gets what he wants, he feels his impact on the world: pretty powerful stuff for a one-year-old.

A thirteen-month-old might pull Dad's pant leg in the direction of the toy shelf, raise both arms to be picked up, and point to his favorite truck, saying "Uhh" with some urgency. Dad, the problem-solving partner, responds with hand gestures and asks, "You want something up there?" Joey responds with more "uhh"s and gestures, until Dad picks him up so that he can point to the truck he wants. When this success is repeated many times, Joey learns an important lesson: that small, individual pieces of communication fit together into a big pattern and can solve problems. Joey gradually strengthens his understanding of patterns (in this case, verbal and nonverbal exchanges) and uses them in an organized way to get what he wants or needs.

This ability for shared social problem-solving begins early and continues with us throughout our lives. Like the earlier levels of interacting and communicating, it is a foundation for all the higher levels of thinking. In fact, it is the beginning of scientific thinking, experimenting, and innovative thinking. Children who are not good problem-solvers often seem disorganized or impulsive, aimless or illogical because they haven't figured out successful ways to express their desires. They can't organize their actions and words to get what they want.

Playful Obstruction

We talked about this strategy when we first discussed Floortime. By playfully getting in the child's way, you encourage him to solve a problem, which you, the challenger, created. Here's an example where Father, faced with a spontaneous uproar, both counterbalances a negative mood to get his daughter communicating and uses another little trick to get her to solve her problem.

Rachel and the Carrots

Sitting in her highchair as dinner begins, twenty-month-old Rachel throws her mashed potatoes on the floor and squawks, "No! No! No!" Struggling to get out of the highchair, she arches her back and shakes her head. A power struggle in the making if Father insists she eat those potatoes (and at this age he is likely to lose). Wanting to counter her negativity, Father chooses a different tack. He imitates her "No" with a playful, enthusiastic shaking of his own head and raising his arms, dancing around a bit, all the while looking puzzled. Then he calmly asks her, "Well, what do you want to eat?" Responding to Daddy's lighthearted but intriguing response, Rachel points to the carrots. Father moves the bowls of carrots and potatoes closer. He mischievously covers up the potatoes with one hand and the carrots with the other. He tells her to point to the one she wants, giving her little peeks under the bowls by quickly moving his hands aside. By now, Rachel is attentive and calm. Her eyes hold a look of anticipation. He plays a little dumb about her choice, encouraging her to express it. She watches Dad's hands and makes her move toward the carrot bowl as he uncovers it one more time. A little smile, a little squeak, and the carrots are hers. Without a fuss, she tries a little potato too. (Admittedly, it isn't always that easy—but sometimes it is.)

Rachel's father deserves some credit. Rachel was not, on the face of it, an easy sell, and yet he offset her negativity with little ado. He avoided the potatoes and refocused her interests, catching her attention. He counterbalanced her fussy mood so that he could begin a "conversation" with her. And then—tah dah!—he play-fully obstructed by making a little game out of Rachel's getting what she wanted, the carrots. Within the context of a peek-a-boo game, he asked her a question with gestures and expressions. He enticed her—a principle of Floortime—by drawing her out of her own mind-set and making her work just a little bit for what she wanted. He didn't just hand over the carrots. He challenged her. He gently got between her and her desire. By offering her a choice, he let her have some control and got her to solve a problem.

This gambit, another kind of Socratic challenge, works equally well with a self-absorbed child who tunes out—a child whose stan-dard mode is one-way communication with himself. You can see why this would be. With a child who completely tunes people out—for instance, one who sits on the floor zooming his racing cars—a father needs to make himself both interesting and involved in the play (but not too intrusive) if he is to get any communication going and strengthen those thinking skills. He can't do as Bradley's mom did because to some degree, he isn't really wanted. He can pretend to be the biggest trash pile in sight, and this type of child will just zoom his cars around him, perhaps barely acknowledging his presence.

Instead, a dad can start out more energized—putting a lot of ex-pression and emotion in his voice and his gestures—when he com-ments on the cool cars or his son's skills at racing. If this doesn't work, he might copy Bradley's mom but more emphatically. He can block a particular path, one foot here, one foot there, making it into a new game. If his child is really finicky, negative, or sensitive, Dad can ask permission while he tries to engage him—"Can we see if the car can get past here, or here, or here?" as he jumps from place to place. If his child says no, Dad has opened one circle, at least, that his son closed. That's a start. With gentle persistence, he and little Zoomer will be problem-solving in no time.

Level Four: Problem-Solving

4a. In a situation where your child needs your help in doing something for him, he . . .

1. Rarely or never uses words or gestures and is therefore not able to let you know what he wants
2. Only sometimes uses words or gestures but often gets frustrated and gives up
3. Is persistent in letting you know what he wants but repeats the same or very similar gestures or verbal directions when you don't understand
4. Is persistent in letting you know what he wants but can modify and change the directions until you understand (that is, your child can keep showing you in different ways what is wanted)

4b. Your child can carry out a series of problem-solving steps, such as finding a certain book, opening it up, turning to a specific page, and looking at the pictures or reading . . .

1. Not at all
2. Sometimes
3. Half the time
4. Most of the time

LEVEL FIVE: MEANINGFUL USE OF IDEAS

Around the age of two, children start to leave the asking-by-pointing stage and try out the asking-with-words stage. Rather than simply pointing to the toy on the shelf and tugging at his father, now thirty-month-old Joey can say what he wants—"Me want toy." The child's emotion invests the symbol (i.e., word) with meaning. Parents expand a child's meaningful use of words by showing interest in their child's opinions and, as he gets older, asking him about everyday situations.

Symbols and Imagination

Once children can use words, they can begin to experiment with imagination. Flights of fantasy take off when a topic is something the child is invested in. If a three-year-old is talking about his favorite foods at dinner, Dad might ask what kind of a food he would create that combines all his favorites. Maybe he would say "pizza applesauce" or "chicken-finger brownies," but whatever, it will be fun and easy for his parents to admire his creativity. For all young children, the wonderful world of pretend indulges their creativity and use of words. With older children, imagination leads into making up songs, telling stories, creating new rules for games, inventing new dance steps, and on and on.

Words and Symbols at School

School can be just as important a spot for creativity and imagination as home. Innovative thinking is the foundation of science, technology, and the arts, and we don't want a focus on rote learning and memorization to undermine this. Your child's ability for abstract thinking and problem-solving, and success as an adult in general, will depend more on creativity than on any other skill. That doesn't mean he gets to ignore the facts, but it does mean that your promoting creativity is vital.

For instance, after learning about animals in Africa, the first-grade teacher can ask the class to come up with ideas about why the elephant sucks up dirt and blows it on his back, why the giraffe has such a long neck, or why lions roar. There are many real reasons and many maybes too, and all children will have some ideas. Or they can go on an imagination expedition and explore what might happen if a gnu had to hop like a kangaroo or an elephant tried to climb a tree. They could imitate how they think it would look. Children first have to understand the facts to do this, but the questions give them permission to think outside the box and have fun with their own ideas.

The same principle applies for an older child, perhaps a sixth grader studying about the Revolutionary War. He learns about the reasons for the war, who won the different battles, and what General Washington did. He learns to use the facts logically, but he also needs to use the facts creatively. A question such as, "If you were a British general at the Battle of Trenton, what would you do differently?" followed by, "Do you think that might have changed the war?" will require imagination. Also, by combining creativity with the facts, the child will remember them much better. If your child has learning problems, creativity is even more important because it will help him figure out his own unique way of remembering facts and understanding concepts.

Good schools and talented teachers already teach this way, as do many parents, but even so, it's not emphasized enough. So, enjoy your child's creative juices, and let his creativity bloom, whether he's a two-year-old on a rocking horse who pretends he's chasing you or a teenager improvising an ongoing saga for her younger siblings each night before bedtime.

Level Five: Meaningful Use of Ideas

5a. When your child reacts to a situation and you ask how he feels, the child . . .

1. Gets confused by what is being asked
2. Finds it hard to respond

3. Is unable to express the feelings with words and instead shows them by hitting, clinging, or getting excited
4. Can describe some feelings (for example, happy or mad) but can't describe other feelings, especially when the emotions are intense
5. Clearly tells you what he feels for a large range of feelings (for example, happy, mad, sad, etc.), even if the feelings are intense

5b. When playing out a make-believe story with friends, your child is . . .

1. Unable to add even basic imaginative ideas
2. Able to develop a few elements of a story, but without elaboration, motivations, or feelings
3. Sometimes able to suggest a new story line with motives and emotions
4. Almost always able to create a story line with motives and emotions

5c. When you ask your child his opinion about something, he is . . .

1. Unable to share any thoughts or opinions
2. Rarely able to share thoughts or opinions
3. Sometimes able to respond to the question with an opinion
4. Almost always responds with opinions and can sometimes initiate them

5d. When your child is playing games or doing other activities with peers, he is . . .

1. Unable to enjoy and share ideas with peers
2. Rarely able to enjoy and share ideas with peers
3. Sometimes able to enjoy and share ideas with peers
4. Almost always able to enjoy and share ideas with peers

LEVEL SIX: LOGICAL THINKING

Susie

> Susie: "I want to go outside"
> Mom: "Why do you want to do that?"
> Susie: "Because I want to play on the swings."
> Mom: "Is that fun?"
> Susie: "Lots of fun."

This is a simple exchange, but extremely important. Susie (three and a half years old) connects her ideas about playing on the swings with Mom's ideas. By answering the idea in a basic "why question," Susie forms a logical thought process. (Gradually she'll get through who, what, where, and when too.) Once she gets the hang of it, she can begin to answer why questions about everything in her life, leading the way to understanding how things work and what she feels about them. At a certain stage, why questions may seem to fill every waking hour, with Susie both answering them and asking her own.

More sophisticated causal thinking evolves at each succeeding level. Gradually a child will come to understand how one event leads to another ("The wind blew down my cardboard house"), how ideas operate across time ("If I'm good now, I'll get to go to the park later"), and how ideas operate across space ("Mom isn't here, but she is close by"). Ideas can explain emotions ("I'm happy because I got a toy") as well as organize knowledge of the world. For our little Joey—now a little older—who wants a toy fish on a shelf, it means that his dad can ask why he wants that one, and Joey can answer, "Because it's my favorite." You can see how attaining this level, easily answering why questions, makes the more complex levels of causal thinking and reflection possible.

Creating a Logical Bridge

Sometimes as children begin this new level, they need support to make the leap. Listening for whether your child connects up the ideas in his conversation with yours will let you know if you need to give extra help. For instance, imagine Mom and six-year-old Mikey are talking about school, and Mikey says, "I don't want to talk about school anymore; I want to tell you about my favorite computer game." Mikey wanted to change the subject, and he created a logical bridge to do it.

Mom can answer, "Oh, okay. What's your favorite computer game?" or alternatively, "We'll talk about that in a minute. First, finish telling me about what your teacher said today." Mikey, as with any child, certainly needs Mom to be there as a reciprocal partner, but he connects ideas quite well and makes transitions.

On the other hand, take Jessica, who is talking to Mom about school and suddenly shifts the topic to a cartoon figure. So Mom says, "Whoa, Jessica! You were telling me about your teacher, how he didn't let you read, and now you're talking about Buzz Lightyear—I'm lost!" She brings her child back and helps her make the connection.

If Jessica says, "Oh, I don't want to talk about my teacher anymore, I want to talk about Buzz," Mom can say, "Oh, okay, I didn't understand. We can talk about Buzz, but why do you want to talk about him instead of your teacher?"

"Oh, because the teacher yelled at me today." By challenging her child to make sense, she helps her connect her ideas together. Jessica needs to practice and over time learn to make these connections on her own. If a child needs help with making connections, it is crucial in any conversation with missing links for Mom to intervene—to pay close attention and pull the child back to the topic.

Why is this so crucial? Because being logical is important above and beyond answering why questions about needs and wishes. It is the basis for our daily lives.

When a child talks about something and suddenly drifts off into make-believe, with no link, what is really happening here? He is actually avoiding a subject that makes him nervous. He is escaping into fantasy. Fantasy is good, but *not* when it is an unconnected escape from difficult topics. When your child changes the topic in midstream or says something seemingly out of left field, you can challenge the shift by acting confused. Questions or mock confusion block the nonlogical escape path and reconnect to the logical one. The more often a child uses this avoidance technique, the more diligently parents need to guide the child back to logical thinking.

Logic and Reality

Connecting ideas logically is the basis for understanding reality. To discriminate between what is real and what is not, to make judgments about what is going on, the child needs to compare experiences inside himself with those outside and to categorize which are fantasy and which are reality. His ongoing interactions with you support this distinction because they continuously put a "me" in contact with a "not-me." Recognizing who is "not-me" provides an external reality, one outside the child. Thus, "reality testing" requires an ability to organize a sense of self that is distinct from one's sense of others. Such reality testing is a critical foundation for logical thinking, which in turn leads to a cascade of new skills, including those involved in reading, math, writing, debating, and scientific reasoning. Without logical thinking, facts are often used to support irrational beliefs.

Emotions and Logical Thinking

At each new thinking level, children need to pull in and reexperience the full range of emotions. At the level of logical thinking, it is of particular importance. Here is the beginning of developing emotional reality: learning to understand and express one's own emotional reactions, learning to distinguish the nuances of emotion in another person, and in the process keeping the two untangled. When a child can bring logical insights to bear on the emotions swirling around him, he will grasp his own situation better and gain a more grounded perspective on the future.

Having a feeling can be very different from expressing and understanding a feeling. Most people—adults and children—have the full range of feelings, but some don't express them all because they can't. When a child can't use creative and logical thinking to express feelings, those feelings don't go away. Instead, they continue to exist in a more global form, sometimes a catastrophic form. A child can't reflect upon and deal with a feeling that he can't express.

Does your child explain and make sense of all his feelings? Can he talk about why he's sad as well as why he's happy, angry, or scared? Or does he just talk about being angry and never about being happy, or vice versa? Or does he just give you global answers such as, "I feel good" or "I feel bad," but can't describe specific emotions? In his pretend play does he include such emotions as excitement, enthusiasm, joy, fear, anger, and competitiveness—"Mr. Troll is going to get you!" or, "Barney needs a hug." Can he let all his feelings out, in play and in everyday situations?

There may be many reasons why a child is not in touch with a feeling, but for some feelings, it is more obvious than others—anger, for instance.

Discussing Anger

Everyone gets angry. But many people have problems expressing anger constructively. Parents who are uncomfortable with anger and inhibit it usually don't want their child's play to involve anger, they don't want their child to be angry, and they themselves don't want to discuss anger. If parents try to keep anger under the carpet, out of sight, because it's a "bad" feeling, the child has only two choices in an angry moment: 1) to explode and lose control; or 2) to contain the emotion.

We have all witnessed explosive anger and the destruction it can cause. Containment is less easy to identify. The child who contains and inhibits anger tends to be passive and generally cautious about life in order to keep the feeling under control. This can lead to other problems—physical symptoms such as stomach aches and pains, skin rashes, and headaches as well as depression or ritualistic behavior such as compulsions and obsessions. Children who face a parent's explosive anger may be too frightened to express their own and decide that containment is safer.

Anger exists—not expressing it doesn't get rid of it. Getting mad is part of the human condition. Rather than act it out or bury it, we want to socialize anger and make it constructive and manageable. We want to make it something the child can express. To do that, we first have to allow expressions of anger when communicating together. With a nonverbal toddler we can show that instead of banging, biting, or hitting, he can signal his anger with a grimace, a yell "Arggh!" or with an angry movement of his arm. You can then ask (which includes your gestures too), "What's the matter?!" and he can gesture back. Eventually, at the next thinking level, this exchange evolves into the child using words, "Me angry."

When a child begins to think logically, a favorite toy becomes a pawn for emotional expression. For instance, Dad can ask Bobby's alligator, who (with four-year-old Bobby's help) is aggressively biting Dad's leg, "Mr. Alligator, why are you biting me?"

Then Bobby can say, "Mr. Alligator is mad," leading Dad to ask why that is so. "He wants to play outside," says Bobby. Sometimes it's easier for children to express an emotion—especially the negative ones or ones they are anxious about—through a toy. It's less threatening.

When an older child is pretty good with emotions at the logical stage, Mom can ask directly, "Why are you so mad today?" "You didn't let me watch my TV shows." And Mom says, "You thought you should be able to?" "Yes, I did!" "Where did you get the idea that you can watch six hours of TV a day?" The start to a contentious discussion, no doubt, but if there is some respect for each other's opinion, it can be a discussion that includes all the thinking levels—attention, engagement, two-way communication, problem-solving, meaningful use of ideas—including logically connected ideas. You'll know you've done a good job when, at a later age, your child bests you in the discussion.

With all basic feelings, including "negative" ones, children can learn to express them using the thinking skills at their command. The ultimate goal is for children to integrate the range of emotions into each level of thinking. Eventually they will reach the highest level described below, where they can reflect thoughtfully about these emotions. If a child avoids a certain emotion, you can help him include it by "stirring the pot" *gently*.

For instance, some children never want to lose. Even in make-believe, they take their creative play very literally. It's not really pretend; it's too stuck in reality. You can use fantasy to explore a child's concerns about competing and losing, creating conflict in pretend play—your toy car races the child's or your car gets in the way of the child's so his car can't win—both to stir healthy assertiveness and competitive juices, just a little at a time. Or you say with a light, teasing laugh, "My ballerina is a better dancer than yours!" Because avoidance signals some discomfort with the emotion, the child may get nervous so, again, stir gently. After awhile, when your child is a bit more comfortable competing, you can raise the subject directly but supportively, "Why don't you like that? What makes you so uncomfortable when you lose?"

Level Six: Logical Thinking

6a. When your child feels emotional (good or bad) toward you, he . . .

1. Is unable to tell you why he feels the way he does
2. Can partially tell you how he feels, but the explanation wanders and is hard to understand
3. Can give you a clear reason for some feelings, such as happiness, but not others, such as anger or frustration
4. Can give you a clear reason for why he feels a certain way for most feelings
5. Can give you a clear reason for why he feels a certain way, even under stress or with extreme emotions

6b. How often is your child able to engage in pretend play or games with peers in which the story, drama, or imaginative game makes sense (i.e., follows a logical sequence or story line)? My child . . .

1. Is unable to be imaginative with another person and make sense
2. Can be imaginative infrequently with another person and make sense
3. Sometimes can be imaginative with another person and make sense
4. Almost always can be imaginative with another person and make sense

6c. Is your child able to enjoy and sustain friendships? My child . . .

1. Is unable to develop friendships with peers
2. Is able to develop friendships infrequently, and they are not close
3. Is sometimes able to enjoy close friendships with peers
4. Is almost always able to enjoy and sustain close friendships with peers

5

Building Advanced Thinking

By three or four years of age, a child's personality starts to sparkle. Out come the likes and dislikes, good and bad moods, and a verbal relationship with you. Those early days, when she was crawling and cooing at you, when you wondered who really was in there, are fading. You, as a parent, have a good inkling of who she is. She now tells you—even when you don't ask. In these later years, you get to be the slightly confused playmate in need of direction, with whom your child will create a splendid drama with emotion, movement, and a rich sensory palette.

During the next levels, your child will develop logic, more subtle and complex ideas, more nuanced emotional reactions, and a secure knowledge of who she is. Just hearing a child explain what she likes or why she doesn't want to do something, you can feel proud about how thoughtful and insightful she is becoming, even when she disagrees with you. Again, at the end of each level of thinking is a series of questions to help you gauge your child's comfort with the new thinking process and determine what experiences and support your child needs to make the weaker areas into strengths.

LEVEL SEVEN: MULTICAUSAL THINKING

Between ages four and five, your child is ready to give multiple reasons for an action or a feeling. The simpler logical thinking of the previous level—answering why questions with one reason—is the foundation. Multicausal thinking takes being logical one step further. When Mom asks three-and-a-half-year-old Benjamin, who is just beginning to answer why questions, "Why do you want to watch that DVD?" he'll say, "Because I like it." He connected his idea to Mom's, but even with further prompting, he'll leave it at that. On the other hand, his six-year-old sister Julie may give her Mom the exact same answer, but with Mom's follow-up, "Why this particular one?" Julie spills out multiple reasons. "The girl in it is cool. She gets to solve the mystery. And I really like her friends." She is opening a real discussion with the potential for many questions and opinions.

In spontaneous, ordinary conversation, your child naturally practices multicausal thinking, mostly without your prompting. If a child gets stuck for an answer, you can suggest possibilities and have her choose. Here, the rule is always to give the desirable choice first and the weak or undesirable choice last. This way, the child can't take the easy way out by just repeating the last thing you say. So, if mom asks her six-year-old daughter why she chose a particular DVD and she says she likes it—end of conversation— Mom can be genuinely curious. "No other reasons?" If she answers, "I don't know," Mom can offer, "Well, gee, do you want to watch it because it's about Aladdin and Jasmine or because it's scary?"

"Oh, silly, Aladdin and Jasmine. I like them!" Even though Mom supplies the options, her child still has to think to give her an answer.

And as long as she has her attention, she can go for another round: "Why do you like Aladdin and Jasmine so much?"

"I don't know."

"Do they do lots of exciting stuff or do they sit around?"

"Oh, they do really cool stuff." Once again, the child thinks about the reason that makes sense to her.

This isn't a test session. It is a time for parents to show simple curiosity and enthusiasm about a child's interests, which, by the way, encourages her to think through many ideas and reasons, something she can do but maybe not completely on her own. This is an opportunity to follow a child as she changes and grows.

Multicausal Thinking and Emotions

Social relationships give us a grand opening to ask questions about feelings. It can be as simple as being curious about your daughter's reasons for wanting to play with one friend instead of another:

Nicole's Feelings

Mom: "Who do you want to have over to play today?"

Nicole: "Let's call Jennifer."

Mom: "Why Jennifer?"

Nicole: "She's fun. We like the same games."

Mom: "Oh, that's nice. What do you play?"

Nicole: "Well, we both like to play the same computer game."

That's one causal answer. Mom can challenge Nicole to come up with more.

Mom: "So, what else do you like about Jennifer?"

Nicole: "She's nice. We like to talk together, and she tells me secrets."

Mom: "Ah, yes, you two always seem to be giggling. Must be good secrets. Lots of fun for you?"

Nicole: "Yes, I'd really like her to come over."

Some children come up with two or three reasons; some give you five or six. Gradually, by your showing interest, the two or three will expand to five or six, creating space for deeper feelings to surface.

Children provide parents ample opportunity for getting into the realm of feelings. For the child who looks a little glum, Mom can ask, "Why are you looking so sad today, sweetheart?" and then find out that the kids were mean. Asking what happened, she hears, "They picked me last for softball and made fun of my haircut." Or with a child who is irritable and a little snappy, Mom can ask, "Sweetheart, you look like you're ready to bite someone's head off. How come?" and learn, "I have lots of homework, and I hate homework!" Going after more reasons, "Is there anything that happened today?" you find out that "Susie said my shoes look funny." Of course, you also want to ask about positive feelings: "You sure are in a good mood today! Anything special?" "Well, there was a birthday party at school, and we had cupcakes." "That's cool! Anything else?" and of course, there are many things.

Feeling insecure or uncomfortable with certain feelings can undermine this level fairly easily and introduce reactions that are counterproductive, namely being an all-or-nothing thinker. For instance, take a person who gets frustrated by an activity and responds, "I'm so stupid." Or a person who disagrees with someone, gets angry, and thinks, "I hate that person." If children—and adults too—respond to a feeling by becoming all-or-nothing thinkers, they can't think through other reasons for the situation and can't analyze the whole spectrum. This narrow response gives little room for improving the situation or gaining an understanding of what caused it. If a learning problem causes insecurity and the response is "I'm just dumb," it's hard to work out a program to overcome the problem. The response stops any conversation, an internal one or one with someone else.

Talking about different feelings—including anxiety—allows a child to apply multicausal thinking to her emotional life and therefore to all aspects of her life.

Multicausal Thinking and Reality

Once a child is comfortable with feelings, she has a greater sense of who she is versus others. Multicausal thinking offers stronger reality testing than just logical thinking. If a child understands the variety of her own feelings, she begins to appreciate those of others and to put her own feelings in perspective. They can be happy, sad, angry, or conflicted ("Well, Mommy, sometimes I like Johnny, but not when he teases me.") And the perspective improves with age. Dad asks twelve-year-old Jenny, "Why do you think Mary didn't play with you today?" and she tells him, "Mary really likes to play soccer, so she hung out with Becky because Becky was picking people for the soccer team. I don't like soccer." "Did it hurt your feelings?" "Well, yes, but she does this sometimes. I think tomorrow she'll want to play again." This is a very sophisticated discussion. Such discussions help the child to think about and know the world she lives in—a world of people with motives, feelings, and social behaviors that may differ from one's own.

The ability to figure out emotions and reactions is critical for social skills and emotional coping. But it has academic benefits too. Appreciating the inner lives of others, the realm of feelings, helps children understand the motives of characters in a novel, figures in history, or those in the news.

Level Seven: Multicausal Thinking

7a. **Is your child able to give you three to five reasons why she likes something (e.g., her favorite video game) or dislikes something (e.g., spinach)? My child is . . .**

1. Unable to give any reasons for her likes or dislikes
2. Able to give one reason if she tries

continues

continued

3. Sometimes able to give multiple reasons, especially if she has strong feelings about the object
4. Able to give many reasons easily

7b. Does your child understand that there may be multiple reasons or feelings causing someone to behave in a certain way? For example, she understands a situation where a friend might be upset with school and is taking out his anger by being mean to your child. Rather than assuming that this friend does not like her, your child is able to consider other possibilities. (This behavior is not expected before age 6.) My child . . .

1. Tends to think in an all-or-nothing way and always personalizes the situation in an extreme way (for example, she says things such as, "He hates me!")
2. Is sometimes able to consider more than one reason for the other person's actions with guidance (for example, someone helping your child think about the multiple reasons for the other person's actions)
3. Is sometimes able to consider multiple reasons for other people's actions on her own
4. Is almost always able to consider multiple reasons for other people's actions

7c. When upset with herself (or alternatively very pleased about something she did), how does your child react? My child . . .

1. Tends to think in an all-or-nothing way. She thinks she is the most stupid, worst, most unpopular, etc., kid around. She emotionally beats herself up
2. Gets very down on herself but can be talked out if it after a lot of effort

continues

continued

3. Gets down on herself and with some effort can talk about the feelings and get more comfortable seeing the situation in context
4. Initially feels bad but is able to talk about her feelings in a fairly balanced way

LEVEL EIGHT: COMPARATIVE AND GRAY-AREA THINKING

The next level is comparative and gray-area thinking, two skills that are closely related and come in consecutively, so we consider them together. Comparative thinking basically calls for using "er"—Mary is nicer, smarter, prettier, taller, etc., than Susie. It involves comparing any two different things. Gray-area thinking means that a child can understand the degrees, or relative influence, of different feelings, events, and phenomena. Mary is almost as smart as Susie, but Lily is the smartest of all.

Comparative and gray-area thinking develop between the ages of six and ten. The big age range occurs because these abilities are, like their very definition, not all or nothing. They mature over the years to become more intricate. Typically, by seven or eight years of age, children start comparing people and things, but being the first child on the block to be a comparative thinker is not significant. What is important is that the child moves in that direction. Many adults, even if they are professionally competent, never develop good comparative and gray-area thinking skills. They live in an all-or-nothing world.

Comparative Thinking

If Mom asks eight-year-old Michael, "Who do you want to invite over today?" Michael may reply, "Oh, I want Mark to come over."

"Why Mark rather than Paul?" To answer that, Michael has to get into comparative thinking. He might say, "Well, because Mark plays basketball better," or, "He likes to kick the soccer ball around, but Paul doesn't." In these answers, he shows that he can compare two different people.

On the other hand, Michael might just answer, "Well, Mark is fun," in which case he's not really comparing Mark to Paul; he's just talking about Mark. Mom can give Michael a little push by saying, "Well, I know that Mark is fun, but why more than Paul?" "Well, Mark likes to play basketball and soccer." "Well, that's great, sweetheart, and I know you like Mark, but I still don't know why you'd rather have Mark than Paul." "Well, Paul doesn't like those games." Now Michael has a reason associated with each choice. He's almost there. One more time around and he will have it. "Let's see—so why do you want Mark more than Paul?" Mom asks again. And Michael says, "Because Mark plays the games I like to play and Paul doesn't." He made it! Or he might just say, "Well, Mark's more fun," or "He's nicer" or "better."

The "He's fun" answer is typical when you first raise a comparative question. For an older child like Michael who, in the latter example, has difficulty with comparative thinking, you want to stay with the subject until the child is really comparing. Try not to be too naggy, just confused and supportive.

Shades of Gray

As we have said, although we don't usually see comparative thinking until six to eight years of age, sometimes we'll see it even in a four- or five-year-old. At whatever age your child can make comparisons, she is then ready to understand the notion of degrees, shades of gray. "Well, how much more fun is Christy than Torie?" "Oh," says five-year-old Jill in a typical response of a younger child, "Lots more 'funner'!" With this kind of answer, Jill is thinking comparatively. Now a straight, more-or-less comparison can be sliced into smaller pieces, creating shades of gray. Mom uses her hands and asks, "Is it this much—a little?" her hands a few inches apart, or "Is it this much—really a lot?" arms extended to the sides, or "Is it kind of in between?" her hands in a medium position. In this way, degrees are demonstrated both visually and verbally. After a couple of times, Jill, with hands flying, can show how much nicer or more fun one friend is than another. This beginning approach to degrees works just as well with expressing her own emotions—how angry or happy or grumpy she is today compared to other days. Children gradually develop a relative sense of quantity.

Seeing shades of gray is very important to your child's emotional and intellectual development. It helps her progress from being a polarized thinker, seeing the world as all black or white, to becoming a more subtle thinker who sees nuances and complexities in relationships, ideas, and people.

In some areas of life, we must have all-or-nothing rules, such as not hurting someone else, but those areas are very few. Intellectual life, as well as emotional life, exists in the gray zone. When children are younger—three and four years old—we expect all-or-nothing thinking and its associated negativism and stubbornness because the child is able to think in terms of only two choices: my way or the highway. Understanding degrees of difference helps that earlier thinking level give way to reason, debate, negotiation, and compromise.

Expanding Gray Area Thinking: Jeremy

How does this capacity for comparative and gray-area thinking expand into the different domains of life? The psychologist Jean Piaget discussed relativistic thinking (i.e., comparative) in school-age children mostly in terms of the visual-spatial world, in understanding relative degrees of quantity—a small ball of string versus a long piece of string; a tall, thin glass of water versus a short, fat one. Here is an example from my clinical practice that illustrates Piaget's concept.

One day I was playing with a young patient named Jeremy. We each built our own forts with different offensive and defensive weapons systems. I said to Jeremy, "I think your laser shield is better than mine. What do you think?" Jeremy, quite pleased to have a better shield, quickly agreed. So I asked him, "Why do you think it's better?" Jeremy said his shield was stronger. Since I wanted to push him to make more comparisons, I asked again, "Yes, but your fort looks different than mine. Does that make yours better?"

"Well," he said, "Mine is bigger, and my laser shield takes up more space. Your laser beams can only go into this little space here." I agreed and playing dumb, asked him how I could make a better laser shield for my fort. Together, we added a ball in front of the fort so that the lasers couldn't knock the door down. When I asked if he thought this was better than before and now as good as his shield, he gave me his ranking—my old fort shield was not good; my new one was okay but still not as good as his.

Jeremy compared the two defense systems and judged their degrees of difference, especially the ones requiring visual-spatial ability. Our game was a two-fer: his reasoning had advanced to a higher level—he applied comparative and gray-area thinking to the visual-spatial world—and, besides that, he was the winner—which is always a good way to end.

As we will see when we discuss the roots of our Learning Tree, you can vary any fun activity to strengthen comparative and gray-area thinking. You and your child can try out different hiking trails and decide if one is harder than the other. Or you can set up your own obstacle courses, try them out, and compare them. This kind of practice prepares children for academics and then work. Adults need to be able to compare two forms of government, to analyze cultural patterns in different countries, or to evaluate the subtleties of an office planning process as well as the nuances of city politics. Shades of gray exist in all the arenas of life.

Gray-Area Thinking and Emotion: Michael

Piaget's insights into relativistic thinking and the visual-spatial world are extremely important for understanding a child's development. But this kind of thinking can reach into all realms of life—motor, sensory, and emotional. The emotional world received little attention by Piaget. Our work has shown that underlying all the child's cognitive abilities is emotional development. The child first learns more advanced ways of thinking through how she applies and uses her emotions in ever more complex ways. Let's go back to Michael, who wants to invite Mark over rather than Paul. It seems that there are more reasons than just a difference in sports interests.

Later on, Michael explains to his mother, "Mark almost always plays with me when I ask him, but Paul only plays with me when his other friends are busy, so I think he really doesn't like me that much." Here, Michael offers a rather eloquent distinction.

Mom can help Michael figure out his feelings around this comparison by asking, "How does this make you feel?"

"Mad, but a little sad too. But I don't feel as sad when my other friends are around to play with me."

Michael's insight into degrees of feeling goes further.

"How mad do you get?" his mother asks.

"Well, a little." (Michael holds out his hands with about four inches between them.) "I kind of want to get even. Sometimes when he wants to play, I want to say no, just to make him feel bad."

Michael is comfortable with his feelings and is also realistic. He can distinguish the degree to which he's sad and angry. He is at home with gray-area thinking.

If children (or adults) are not comfortable with certain feelings, they won't be able to see the shades of gray. Similar to our discussion at the level of multicausal thinking, not seeing degrees of certain emotions can develop into a problem of all-or-nothing thinking. This is more likely to occur with negative emotions, such as anger, sadness, rejection, or frustration, but some children may need just as much support to talk about degrees of positive feelings—happiness and joy—as well. If they see shades of gray with some emotions but not others, this level will be unstable. In Chapter 15 we discuss the role anxiety can play in learning challenges and ways to handle it.

Level Eight:
Comparative and Gray-Area Thinking

8a. **Is your child able to make simple comparisons between objects, toys or books, for instance? For example, "I like Harry Potter better than I like Spiderman." (This behavior is not expected before age eight.) My child is . . .**

   1. Unable to make simple comparisons
   2. Able to make comparisons if really interested in one of the objects
   3. Sometimes able to make comparisons
   4. Always able to compare between objects.

8b. **Is your child able to distinguish the varying degrees of different feelings for one situation (gray-area thinking)? For example, if participating in a new activity (soccer game, piano**

continues

continued

recital), she can both express excitement in doing a new thing and be a little afraid of not performing well? My child is . . .

1. Not yet able to distinguish varying degrees of different feelings for one situation
2. Able to understand and express varying degrees of feelings some of the time with guidance (for example, someone helps your child think about the varying degrees of different feelings)
3. Able to express varying degrees of feelings for a situation some of the time on her own
4. Able to express varying degrees of feelings for a situation most of the time

8c. **Is your child able to describe varying degrees of feelings to compare different friends? For example, "I like Jennie more than Julie, but my neighbor Anne is my most favorite friend." My child is . . .**

1. Not yet able to use gray-area thinking to make comparisons in peer relationships
2. Only infrequently able to use gray-area thinking to make comparisons in peer relationships
3. Often able to use gray-area thinking to make comparisons
4. Almost always able to use gray-area thinking to make comparisons

LEVEL NINE: REFLECTIVE THINKING (THINKING OFF AN INTERNAL STANDARD)

The highest level, reflective thinking—also called thinking off an internal standard—usually begins to develop between ages nine and thirteen. It allows a child to evaluate her own behavior, thoughts,

and feelings and is essential for all relationships as well as advanced
academic activities. Reflective thinking is "thinking about thinking." It is your ability to think about yourself and judge yourself and
your own performance. It gets stronger from the early adolescent
years up through the adult years as the complexities of life add new
experiences to reflect on. But many adults don't fully master this
level—a detriment to them academically, career-wise, and socially.
The ability to reflect, to judge oneself in the context of one's relationships and interactions with others, is a critical ability. It is basically this feedback loop, a self-critical analysis, that lets us learn from
experience by putting each experience in the proper perspective.

An Internal Standard

To reach this level, one needs an internal standard developed
through life's experiences. New experiences or emotions are then
evaluated against this standard of sense of self. To establish this
standard, there has to be a "me" or a "self"—a "me" who has an
opinion, a "self" who makes judgments. If a teenager can say, "I left
that homework until the last minute, so no wonder I got it wrong"
and "That isn't like me," she shows this kind of self-reflection. The
more experience adolescents or adults have—with education, jobs,
cultures, people—the broader their context to reflect, compare,
and judge. Most twelve-year-olds have a limited context because of
fewer relationships or experiences and so can do only a bit of reflective thinking, but it is a beginning.

Self-Evaluation: Home and School

A child's reflective thinking develops through her self-awareness.
Parents can ask her opinions about relationships, academics, and
current events, even if these opinions are still in formation: "Why
do you think your friend Joe is zealous of John?" "Why did you like

The Outsiders better than *Catcher in the Rye?*" "For whom would you vote for president?" Your respect for and interest in her opinions will make your child feel valued. She will want to give you not only more opinions but also more thoughtful ones.

When you solicit your child's opinions, challenge her to defend them. Facts need to support opinions. If Dad asks, "Well, what do you base that statement on?" his child has to recruit the facts: she has to study, read, or actually go witness relevant activities or events. Rather than letting her get by with a simple opinion, Dad challenges the child to build a case. For example, she may be able to explain why J. K. Rowling is a good writer, but has she read J. R. R. Tolkein or C. S. Lewis? The more authors she reads, the broader is the context for her opinion.

Some children are not good at remembering facts. This does not limit their ability to form sound opinions because facts have shaped their ideas. Becoming a strong reflective thinker will help them recognize when their opinions need more examination and support. When they need to gather or check facts, they have reference books and the Internet at their fingertips. The same goes for children who are poor at grammar and spelling. If they are reflective, they will know when they need to ask for help. As for children who have good ideas but poor writing skills, they can learn many techniques, which we explain later, to organize their thoughts and map out essays. But without reflective thinking abilities, they won't know when they need to do this.

The broader children's academic and learning experiences, the more they can apply reflective abilities in intellectual areas. The wider their social circles, the easier it will be for them to reflect on their choices of friends. One can't really become a good reflective thinker without swimming about in different subjects and different worlds. By challenging your child to try new books, hobbies, friends, sports, and musical instruments and to express her opinions on each, you will encourage a truly reflective thinker.

Abstract Thinking

Abstract thinking means using one's personal perspective for insight and then introducing those insights into a different, abstract context. True abstract thinking is being able to think to oneself, "Well, let's see. What if someone said that to me? What would I do? I'd get mad. But she's different—she isn't as sensitive as I am. So she takes it in stride and doesn't pay much attention to it." This way, we use insight about ourselves and others to generate an abstract perspective. Breaking it down helps a child to go back and forth between the personal and the abstract and become a truly reflective thinker.

Having an experience and assuming that everyone has the same reaction to it as you do is not abstract thinking. People who do that personalize everything; they get lost in their own perspective: certain things make *them* angry; therefore, everyone would be angry in the same situation.

Reflection means having a sense of who you are and being able to compare other experiences to your own in a logical and realistic manner.

Level Nine: Reflective Thinking

9a. Does your child know herself well enough to be able to judge how she is feeling or responding to a given situation? For example, your child can evaluate her own feelings or behaviors by making judgments such as, "I feel angrier than I should." (This behavior is not expected before age 11 to 12.) My child is . . .

1. Unable to judge how she is feeling or responding to a given situation

continues

continued

2. Sometimes able to judge how she is feeling with guidance
3. Able to judge how she is feeling and responding some of the time on her own
4. Able to judge how she is feeling and responding most of the time

9b. Is your child able to fully engage in peer friendships and at the same time have her own opinions about herself and others? My child is . . .

1. Unable to be fully engaged in peer friendships and have her own opinions
2. Rarely able to be fully engaged in peer friendships and have her own opinions
3. Sometimes able to be fully engaged in peer friendships and have her own opinions
4. Almost always able to be fully engaged in peer friendships

9c. Is your child forming and beginning to use her own inner ideas about what's right and wrong (values)? My child is . . .

1. Unable to form and use her own inner values
2. Rarely able to form and use her own inner values
3. Sometimes able to form and use her own inner values
4. Almost always able to form her own inner values

THE THINKING LEVELS AT SCHOOL

These last two chapters are full of examples of what parents can do at home to help their children develop the thinking levels. Before the children have climbed to the top of the thinking levels or even mastered the ones they have experienced, though, they are off to school. The development of these thinking levels continues there. That's what the three Rs are about, right? Not entirely, especially if your child has some learning problems.

As you have seen and will be reminded of in later chapters, thinking—as well as becoming a better thinker—isn't primarily about learning facts. It's about mastering senses, movement, and emotions. Ideally, school experiences will help a child keep all these factors working together.

Meanwhile, in the next chapter we will see a real-life school situation in which children use and develop all the thinking levels that we have just described.

THE TREE TRUNK IN SUMMARY

As we have seen over the last two chapters, from a developmental point of view, intelligence is the progressive transformation of our emotions to produce more mature thinking abilities. Said another way, each transformation builds higher levels of thinking and intelligence into a view of the world where each sense and emotion is strongly developed and integrated with the rest. These levels of thinking are a framework for analyzing and understanding a child's developmental profile. With this information, therapists and parents can help a child with learning problems.

In our work with professionals, we call this framework the DIR Model or, more formally, the Developmental, Individual-Difference, Relationship-Based Model. Here, "developmental" refers to the functional developmental (i.e., thinking) levels described above; "individual-difference" refers to the child's unique processing profile; and "relationship-based" looks at the child's relationships and how they can support enhanced development. Now used by those who work with children in many disciplines, the DIR Model gives important insight into understanding a child's development.

In summary, the thinking levels that compose the tree trunk are:

1. Attention (develops in the first days of life): Calm interest and purposeful responses to sights, sound, touch, movement, and other sensory experiences.

2. Engaging the world (develops between two and five months): Growing expressions of intimacy and relatedness.

3. Interaction and communication (develops between four and ten months): A range of back-and-forth interactions, with emotional expressions, sounds, hand gestures, and the like, to convey intentions.

4. Shared problem-solving (develops between ten and eighteen months): Many social and emotional interactions in a row used for problem-solving.

5. Meaningful use of ideas (develops between eighteen months and three years): Ability to use meaningful words or phrases and interactive pretend play with caregivers or peers.

6. Logical thinking (develops between three and four and a half years): Logical connections between meaningful ideas.

7. Multicausal thinking (develops between four and six years): Ability to give multiple reasons for a feeling or idea.

8. Comparative and gray-area thinking (develops between six and ten years): Ability to describe degrees of difference in feelings, relationships, and objects.

9. Reflective thinking (develops after nine years and continues to develop throughout life): The ability to evaluate and reflect on feelings, oneself, and events in the world.

6

Using All the Thinking Levels
The Sidwell Friends Buddy Project

By Richard Lodish, Ed.D., with Barbara Szoradi

The third-graders at the Sidwell Friends School in Washington, DC, have a buddy system with the pre-K and kindergarten students. The children in the higher grades befriend the younger ones who are, in the case of the pre-K students and many of the kindergartners, new to the school. Many schools have versions of this system, all of which are valuable to children. The little kid gets to have a big kid (cool by the definition of any five-year-old) as his friend and playmate, meet other older kids, and maybe even join in one of their games. The younger child may think he has just gone to kindergarten heaven.

Barbara Szoradi, the third-grade teacher who organizes this project, adds an extra ingredient. Before meeting their buddies and throughout the rest of the year, the third-graders have practice sessions with their teachers where they role-play and discuss what they think will happen, what kinds of problems will occur, and what they should do in particular situations. The teachers set the tone by explaining to them, "You are like a combination older brother or sister and babysitter to your buddy. Your job is to make sure they have a wonderful time and learn from your good example." They know that they can't run off to shoot hoops or be part of the rivalry in the soccer game, for awhile anyway. They have to find out what their buddy wants to do—to get the child's attention and to engage him in a welcoming spirit to the school.

This can be a rather daunting task for an eight- or nine-year-old. What if the younger child doesn't want to talk, is scared, tries to run away from them, or suddenly launches into a dangerous activity? The third-graders know the possibilities. They've been there and not so long ago. Here, in the pre- and post-practice sessions, is where they engage with their teachers and other classmates and establish their own rhythm of relating. Here is where they get to problem-solve with each other and the teacher using words, feelings, and gestures. Here is where they get to figure out multiple reasons why the kindergartners may act a certain way. Maybe they are nervous, shy, or as one child aptly put it, "afraid of someone who is so much taller."

One challenge the teachers offer to the children is to try to understand the younger child's emotions—that is, to read the social and emotional cues, not only words but also gestures, to know whether the younger one is happy or sad, feeling friendly and welcomed, or uncomfortable but not saying so. Not only do they have to encourage the kindergartners to engage with them, they have to engage with the kindergartners and focus on them to understand what is going on. In the practice discussions, the teachers ask the third-graders specifically about reading these subtle cues. The children learn to be aware of these observations and to put them into words. The peer group discussion lets them learn from each other because it involves a lot of reciprocal conversation, problem-solving, and reflection.

Needing to know how to manage these potential tests to their new responsibility gives the children tremendous motivation to be self-reflective, even though they are still a little young to indulge fully in this thinking level.

On rainy days, the third-graders read picture books to their buddies. Even the older children with reading problems feel successful telling the story from the picture book. One of the teachers said about those rainy days, "To observe a room full of four-year-olds snuggling against or in the lap of a third-grader is a special sight."

During the year, the third-graders keep notebooks about their experiences. In these pages, they relive the events with humor, horror, and pretend disbelief. They talk about their own emotion around interactions with their buddy, and they sometimes even describe how they see the causes and effects. As a teacher noted, "When students write in their notebooks about their young buddies, it often takes them to a different level with their writing."

It takes them to a different level in their thinking as well. This kind of experience allows children to practice, enrich, and master all the levels of thinking. Such is the power of learning through thinking with emotional connections.

PART THREE
THE ROOTS

Marilyn Nolt

Getting to the Roots
Avoiding Labels

Parents of children with learning disabilities frequently hear labels such as "Attention Deficit/Hyperactivity Disorder/Attention Deficit Disorder" (ADHD/ADD), "nonverbal learning disabilities," or "dyslexia." What do these labels really mean, and what can you really do about them?

Take dyslexia. It is defined as difficulty in reading. Past that, you get one set of symptoms from the medical community, another from the federal government, and still others from various textbooks written by experts. Some experts bring in early delayed speech; others focus on reading and spelling problems. At the end of the day, what you have is a general label that indicates a reading problem. It says nothing about the cause. It's somewhat like bringing your child who has swollen glands to the pediatrician. She gives you a diagnosis of lymphadenopathy. What is a lymphadenopathy? Swollen glands. Until you know why the glands are swollen, the treatment is guesswork.

"Nonverbal learning disorder" is another global classification. The label refers to learning problems in such areas as math; puzzle solving;

fast, complex movements; reading maps and graphs; and having a sense of one's environment—things that don't require verbal reasoning, auditory processing, or comprehension of words and sounds. This problem is on the right side of the brain—spatial and motor planning capacities and some emotional capacities—rather than the left side of the brain—verbal learning. Again, it is a fine term for indicating that a problem exists, but it doesn't lead to a treatment.

The way to improve ADHD or dyslexia or a nonverbal learning disorder is to distinguish the underlying problems. These problems originate from the sensory system. In our tree metaphor, these are the roots that nourish the tree trunk, our thinking levels. The solution to these problems comes from figuring out how a child uses different sensory systems and then piecing together a sensory-specific profile of the child's learning strengths and weaknesses.

Each child has a unique profile. A child may have a very strong visual memory—if you show her a series of cards, she'll readily remember the pictures and the words written under them—but poor visual-spatial processing—if you ask her to draw the mirror image of a picture of a house, she won't be able to. Some children may have motor problems but be very good with abstract visual problem-solving—the stereotypical absentminded professor who visualizes space and sees complex relationships but is very clumsy. The weaknesses help explain how the problem came to be; the strengths will provide many of the tools for improving the weaknesses.

Keep in mind these four points:

- The sensory system—the roots—is crucial for well-developed thinking;
- Therefore, problems in the sensory system can undermine our ability to think;
- Many sensory deficits can cause the same symptom or problem;
- And one particular deficit can cause more than one problem.

For the next few pages I want to use one specific label, inattention, or ADD, to illustrate these points, namely: 1) how this one difficulty can result separately from problems in different sensory systems; and 2) how one sensory pathway or root (such as sound) can cause inattention in multiple ways, depending on what part of the system has a glitch.

Your appreciation of these relationships is important. You are the best observer of your child. If your child can decode sensations and then integrate them—using all of her senses, her motor skills, her language, and her visual-spatial understanding of the world— she will find it easy to pay attention and solve problems. And you'll automatically see that. If, on the other hand, her mental/physical "team" doesn't mesh well, she will live in a more piecemeal world and will have a harder time. You'll see that too. Your grasp of how it all fits together will allow you to help your child pay attention and keep developing intellectually and emotionally.

INATTENTION AS A SYMPTOM

Inattention is not considered a learning problem per se, but it certainly does get in the way of learning. Here is a typical situation:

The phone rings. The exasperated voice on the other end tells Mom that her son Billy squirms, fidgets, talks to neighbors, and doesn't listen to the teacher. He doesn't pay attention. Not only that, but his antics interrupt the children around him, and so they don't pay attention either. The caller—it could be a teacher, guidance counselor, principal, or whoever—mentions "attention deficit disorder" or "attention deficit/hyperactivity disorder" and puts the burden on Mom. She has to do something. Of course, Mom has tried; she's already talked with Billy, but obviously with little impact. So what can she do?

First, this mom, or any parent, needs to look beyond the symptoms—in this case, not paying attention.

There are two ways to think about attention. One way is to simply consider it a feature of the human nervous system. Either you can pay attention or you can't. And if you can't, you can take a stimulant medication, such as Ritalin, Adderall, or Concerta, to improve your focus. In this version, inattention is something you have. You get rid of it by taking medication.

The other way to think about attention is that it is a learned process that develops gradually. In the first months of life, as we saw, when a baby turns toward Mommy's voice or looks at Daddy's face and gives a big smile, that's the beginning of attention. When a toddler turns and points to a teddy bear that she wants, that gestural problem-solving uses attention. When a child sits in the classroom listening to the teacher's instructions and then raises her hand to ask a question, that uses attention. Whether a child follows an object as in the first instance, uses the motor system to solve a problem as in the second, or communicates as in the last one—it involves paying attention.

Together with many of my colleagues who work with children with attentional problems, I think about attention as a dynamic, active process simultaneously involving many parts of the nervous system. In our version, attention includes taking in sights, sounds, and touch; processing information; and planning and executing actions. It is not about how long a child can sit still. Many successful professors, engineers, doctors, teachers, chefs, school principals, and wonderful parents constantly fidget. Whether or not people fidget, if they can absorb information, process and comprehend it, and plan and execute actions, they can pay attention.

So if inattention is not just a nervous system glitch that you fix with a pill, what is it and what causes it? How can you fix it?

For the most part, inattention is a symptom of other problems. It's like having a fever. Obviously, a fever is not a disease but a symptom common to many. Taking a pill to get rid of a fever without looking for the cause is not good medicine. You need to understand what is going on. So where do you look to figure out what causes inattention? Because this chapter introduces the sensory systems, that's a smart guess. But why? What does seeing, hearing, feeling—all the roots in our tree metaphor, all the different ways in which we take in, comprehend, and convey information—have to do with a child being inattentive?

Processing Sounds

Many a parent whose child has attentional problems has experienced something like the following. Dad says to Anna, "I need you to go upstairs, put on your shoes, come back down, and get ready to go because we're going out to lunch." Awhile later, usually longer than Dad thinks it should take, Anna comes back downstairs—minus the shoes. Dad says, "Where are the shoes? What have you been doing? Didn't you pay attention?" Dad is aggravated and tells her to go back and get them. Anna shrugs and mumbles something. She goes upstairs and this time brings them back. Why didn't she do it the first time? Was she just not listening? It certainly feels that way to Dad. But it isn't.

As I mentioned above, inattention is just the symptom. In Anna's case, the problem is how she processes a particular sensation—sounds—that is, decoding the distinct sounds that make up words. Clinicians call it an auditory processing problem, of which there are a few different forms. Anna's is a fairly common variety: she can't hold verbal sequences in mind. She processed the first part of her father's sequence, "I need you to go upstairs," but because she couldn't decode the sounds quickly enough and well enough, the rest became a tangle. She didn't know what to do when she got there. Her problem is in sequencing information—holding onto complex verbal instructions and deciphering them well enough to remember them.

Most of us have stopped a passerby to ask for directions and ended up with our heads spinning. "Drive two blocks, turn right at the light, go three more blocks and pass a church on the left, and then take the second left. The house is the third one on the right after the school." Now suppose that the person has a heavy accent so that you have to think about the words as they spew forth. While you're still "translating'" the first part, he's directed you two miles further down the road through many stop signs and around many corners. Chances are most of us would still be driving around looking for the house. The directions are very clear to the person giving them. He, like most of us, assumes that if he understands them, you will to.

Welcome to the world of a child with auditory processing problems. It's no wonder that Anna, on hearing—for her—a string of hard-to-translate sounds, didn't know what to do. The second time around she had only one instruction, "Go back to get your shoes." She did need to go upstairs, but because that step was a repeat, she could focus on the shoes.

Processing Visual-Spatial Information

Now let's look at another reason for inattention, a different sensory processing problem that involves sight, taking in visual-spatial information. Children who have trouble with this can't take in the whole picture, the entire playing field (literally and figuratively). Details that aren't relevant distract them; they lose their orientation.

A child, let's call him Andy, also has to go upstairs to find his shoes. He goes up, he looks near the bed, and he doesn't see them. As he tries to figure out where else to look (for him it isn't obvious to look in the closet or by the chair), he sees his favorite electric car. Bingo! An immediate distraction. With no mental picture of other places the shoes might be, without being able to hold a picture of the room in mind and eliminate places systematically, Andy can't keep his attention on his task. Of course, he comes downstairs empty-handed or carrying his car. His parents think he didn't listen.

Processing Motor Sequences

Problems processing sounds and sight are common causes of inattention but are not the most prevalent. Of the children who come to see me with attentional problems—with a diagnosis of ADD or ADHD—most have problems with motor planning and sequencing action, another fundamental part of the root system, one that we all use to explore our sensory world. That is, most of them have difficulty organizing and carrying out a multistep action plan in response to a verbal request, visual information, or an implicit demand of the environment, such as getting through an obstacle course. They can't organize the steps, so they don't remember them. The result is that they don't complete the task. (Motor planning problems can also result from neurological differences.)

Mom asks her son, Jonah, to make a peanut butter and jelly sandwich for her. An easy task, right? Well, what does he have to do? He has to go the refrigerator, get out the peanut butter, get out the jelly, put the jars on the table, get the bread from the box, put it on the table, open the cutlery drawer, get a knife, put it with the jars and bread, open the jars, pick up the knife, spread jelly on one piece of bread and peanut butter on the other, put the two pieces together, put the sandwich on a plate, and bring it to her. Sixteen steps. None of them individually seems onerous, but for a child with motor planning and sequencing trouble, all together they are Mount Everest. Jonah is much more likely to end up sitting at the table and licking peanut butter off his fingers than he is to spread it on bread to make the sandwich. Sixteen steps for a child who has problems with planning is a whole lot of organizing—probably too much.

It's the precursor to the child who doesn't quite get the whole homework assignment, doesn't quite do all of what she does get, and then forgets to hand in what she's done. There are too many steps and not enough planning skills.

Regulating Senses

Above are examples of how three different roots cause inattention—sound, sight, and motor planning—because the child has difficulty processing the information that each of these systems pulls in. They aren't the only causes. Children can be inattentive because they have difficulty regulating or modulating a particular sensory system. Some children react to a particular sensation, such as sight, sound, touch, or odor, in a way that makes them disregulated, that is, causes them to be overreactive, underreactive, or to want more sensory input. Children who overreact to a sensation, for instance sound, may get overwhelmed or easily distracted in a noisy room or by a noisy child sitting next to them. For these children, their overreaction leads them to be less attentive. That is one end of the spectrum. At the other extreme are children who don't pay attention because they underreact to sensation—for instance, those for whom a normal speaking voice doesn't register. They are inattentive because they don't notice you.

The other day in my office, I talked in a normal tone of voice to a little boy for at least five minutes before he finally looked up from his toy and noticed me. I had let it go on because I wanted to see how long he could tune out and how underreactive he was. I learned during this session that if I increased the energy in my voice, I could get his attention within a second every time. When his parents gave me his history, I saw that he underreacted to many different stimuli.

Separate from these are other children who seek out sensation. In fact, they often crave it. They constantly look for more touch, more sight, more sound, or more movement. They will be very active, distractible, and inattentive. They are, in fact, the typical children who get diagnosed with ADHD because they are the most obvious. In Chapter 12, we will describe ways children with these various problems regulating senses can be treated.

All that said, there are inattentive children who do not fit any of these descriptions. They have an underlying problem that, as yet, we do not understand.

Part Three describes the developmental pathways for sound, sight, and motor planning and sequencing and addresses how children process these sensations. It also describes how children regulate them. You can follow how the development builds according to age, with some examples for older children. Again we pose questions to help you identify present-day signs that may indicate poorer mastery of an early level for a specific sense—those first six levels we describe in Chapter 4, the breadth and the range of the thinking levels. Using this information coupled with your insights into your child's level of thinking from those two chapters, you can develop a plan. In the last chapter of Part Three, we revisit the problems that faced Sally, the young girl from Chapter 1.

Before reading these chapters, take a minute to ponder two questions: thinking back to when your child was little, which of the areas mentioned above, sound (language and reading), sight (understanding visual space), and motor planning and sequencing (organizing motions) came easily, and which ones were more of a struggle? Were there any indications of over- or underreactions to certain kinds of sounds, touches, tastes, smells, visual details or surroundings, or fast/slow movements? Your reflections will help you focus the information in the following chapters more specifically on your child.

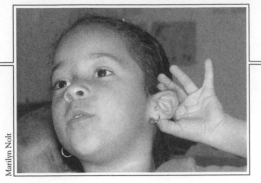

Deciphering Sounds

Distinguishing sounds is the beginning step for developing language, learning to read, and comprehending what is read. At first blush, reading comprehension may seem a bit tangential to sound, but sound recognition, language development, reading, and reading comprehension are a continuum. A child's reading comprehension is no stronger than his ability to recognize words and understand them in context. So in a child who can hear, reading comprehension, as well as the ability to read, depends heavily on auditory processing, that is, how a child takes in and comprehends sounds. Deaf children must rely on what they see—from lipreading, through sign language, and on paper—and may require special instruction to develop word recognition and reading comprehension skills. (In the next two chapters, we will discuss other types of auditory processing problems that are a composite of sensory problems, such as the earlier problem of Anna's fetching her shoes.)

As you read the steps to help your child improve his language skills, keep in mind that labels, such as "verbal learning disability"— used for children who have trouble with decoding sounds, speaking, or reading—may obscure rather than clarify. A child who doesn't distinguish sounds well and is slow to speak may understand a word once he can say it. This problem makes speaking slower but doesn't affect his reading comprehension. Another child may have a good ear and can repeat words but doesn't really understand the meaning. Here a problem with reading comprehension could develop. So as we saw with attention problems, there is not just one reason for a verbal learning disability.

Let's begin by looking (very briefly) at how language first develops.

LANGUAGE DEVELOPMENT

In language development, the newborn's first task is to hear the difference between sounds, that is, to decode them. When we talk baby talk—cooing and making silly faces—we're exposing that baby to different sounds: "Ooh! Aah! You're so sweet. Aren't you cute?" "Boo, boo, ba, ba," emphasizing many different consonants and vowel sounds, being very expressive to draw the baby in. We get really close, and they can't miss the shape of our lips as we say our favorite words (usually either "Ma, Ma" or "Da, Da"). Most babies watch intently and may respond with their own sounds. All of this happens as the baby first takes an interest in the world and in engaging with other people.

When babies reach four or five months of age, sounds become part of an intentional exchange with us. During this two-way communication, babies become active partners so that by eight to ten months, they will reach a crescendo of back-and-forth "goo goos" and "gah gahs," in vocal and physical rhythm with us, arms and legs waving, eyes smiling purposefully. A graceful dance, swaying and vocalizing, with Mom and Dad as partners.

When young children can mimic and create simple sounds, they are ready for the next level in language development—recognizing

patterns. They learn to see that many little pieces (sounds) can create a pattern (a word) that can solve a problem (getting something
of interest). Gradually, preverbal children will use more and more
specific sounds—"bobo," "doh," "bah," forming their own approxi-
mations to represent a bottle, a doll, or a ball—together with gestures. They come to realize that combining specific patterns of
sounds and gestures gets what they want, in other words, solves
their problems.

The first question you might have if your child seems to have a
problem with sounds is, Where do I start? If it's a three-year-old
who can't quite get the hang of talking, you will start at an earlier
thinking level than if it's a six-year-old who's not a natural reader
but talks very well. The three-year-old needs to perceive patterns
and combinations of sounds; the six-year-old needs to connect the
visual image (i.e., letters) with the sound.

Differentiating Sounds

We'll begin with the three-year-old who isn't talking much.

Reading the above description of a baby's development, you
may have had an Aha! moment and now can see exactly where
your child's problem began. But if you didn't, it's OK. Just start the
exercises at the beginning, which for a three-year-old isn't very far
back, and see where your child starts to have a problem.

To begin, you want to animate simple, basic sounds: you rev up to
the "ruh ruh ruh" of "running" or babble the "buh buh buh" of "bat."
See if your child can repeat the sound. Make it into a game with
silly faces and sounds. Exaggerate your expressions, which happens
almost automatically if you increase your energy, so that your child
will watch your face as you make these sounds, even down to the detail of how your tongue and lips move. If he can't distinguish between the "buh" and "duh" sounds, show him how the lips move to

say "buh buh buh," versus how the tongue touches the upper part of the palate for "duh duh duh," then add the "muh" sound. Looking in the mirror, you two can practice the movements and sounds together. (Pat Lindamood, in her well-known Lindamood-Bell approach to reading, emphasizes this aspect.)

With a five-year-old who is still a little shaky with some sounds but has conversations with you, your activity can be more sophisticated, perhaps a funny animal sounds game—you say "dog" then bark, and he copies you; you say "cat" and meow, and he meows, and so on. (Even "Old MacDonald" will do if he still likes it.) If he can already identify animal sounds, you two can take turns making a sound and guessing the animal while repeating the sound. Or maybe a game starts out with your child imitating your animal sound, say a "coo" so you're a "coo coo" bird, and then he gets to try a different bird sound so he's a "dah wah" bird. You can be a "dah mah" bird. If you go back and forth, faster and faster—"dah wah!" "dah mah!" "dah wah!" "dah mah!"—the child hears the sound and repeats it. Then you can throw in a different sound to the pattern—"dah wah!" "dah mah!" "dah wah!" "dah kah!" Kids love to make up their own weird sounds, but the game has to start with the child imitating your sounds.

Producing Sounds: Oral-Motor Challenges

Our main focus in this chapter is children who have problems processing the sounds they hear. When the sound comes in (think of the roots absorbing nutrients), the child can't quite grasp all the parts in order to reproduce them. It's a question of figuring out how to decipher and repeat them. However, children's language skills can also lag because of oral-motor problems, that is, when a child has a hard time moving his tongue, lips, and mouth to make a certain sound. That child may know exactly what sound he wants to make—he has processed the sound properly, he can hear it in his head—he just can't get it out. The muscles in and around his mouth won't take the right shape.

The same type of simple exercises as those above can help children with oral-motor challenges too, but children with oral-motor problems need to start with the easiest sounds, such as "eee, eee, eee," (but experiment, it can vary by child) before moving on to the "buh," "ruh," and "luh" sounds that are harder for the mouth and tongue to control. And remember to exaggerate. The child will get a good workout of the mouth and tongue muscles and will soon have them coordinated. The *Affect-Based Language Curriculum* (ABLC), discussed in Chapter 17, offers additional oral-motor exercises. Speech pathologists and oral-motor specialists have also developed various mouth massage techniques that support movement of the tongue and mouth muscles. These should be done only under the guidance of a speech pathologist experienced in oral-motor work.

Animating Sounds

Once your child is comfortable with different sound sequences, you can add movement. You've already brought in emotion (expression and enthusiasm) to help the child with sounds. Now you add another root, specifically motor planning and sequencing. The child can invent his own arm and body movements to match the sounds he is making; he can be an orchestra leader conducting the sounds; he can dance, wiggle, or jump while singing sounds.

For children who are learning the alphabet, certain letters lend themselves nicely to sounding out the letter while forming it with your body. Take the letter "T," made with a straight body and arms at shoulder height out to the sides, all the while saying, "tee, tee, tee." How about an "oh, oh, oh" by touching your toes, and a "pee, pee, pee" by standing up straight and making your arms into a big circle, holding them in front of your face. You can do all three in a row as fast as possible. (This should feel familiar to those who have sung and formed "YMCA.") If your child is older and learning to spell, you have three different words to work on with these three letters—and spelling, like reading, depends on understanding how sound sequences fit into a pattern. Eventually you'll want to go through all the sounds in the alphabet this way, but you don't have to take the letters in order. I think it's best to start off with those sounds that occur in the words that the child uses the most and then move to the less familiar ones. You'll quickly see that just trying to form certain letters, say a "W" or an "N," will require teamwork and creativity between you and your child.

Differentiating Blends

I favor getting into the blends from the beginning—showing how the letters go together, rather than waiting to master each separately. Start off with the most familiar blends, ones that relate to the child's interests—"tr" if the child loves trucks, for example—so he is emotionally invested. Or if it's winter, do a lot of "brrrr"s outside. Or animal sounds, "grrrr." Then progress to making different blends back and forth, fast, slow, silly, and so on. With a younger or older child, move on to the blends that he needs most in terms of language skills or ones that you know are problematic. Again pull the child in by making the exercises with you fun, expressive, emotive, and filled with movement. For some children, proficiency at perceiving and decoding the sounds will happen quickly; for others, it can take a long time. But with practice, it will happen.

Constructing Words

The next step in language development is putting the pure sounds and blends together into words. So here you are with your three-year-old who is playing with his favorite toy truck. You join his game, showing interest in his toy, saying, "What a great truck." He says "truh," and you interact around the truck, using gestures and movement. You chat about the truck's adventures. Finally he understands the sound pattern well enough to use the full word "truck." Very quickly, he goes from saying "truck," to "my truck" or then "truck here." This play and these verbal leaps can take you and the child off into combining words together into short phrases that involve creative play. As you use words in more complex ways, the child imitates you.

Children seem to learn very rapidly once they see that a pattern of three or four letters creates a word. They are motivated to do this because early in the problem-solving level, they learned that the pattern of making a certain sound and pointing will get them something they want. Consequently, children who are slower at recognizing that sound patterns create words need to work longer on using sounds as part of shared problem-solving, of using sounds and gestures to get something they need or want. Our "Socrates moments" can be a big help. Throughout the day, you can act a little confused when your child utters sounds that are less differentiated. You can gesture and enunciate some choices for him—the real word and a clearly silly word—for what he wishes. To fulfill his wish, he will try his best to repeat the correct word. At that moment he is motivated to try hard, and he does. He doesn't need to be perfect; he just needs to practice, not in a rote, conditioning way, but in an expressive, supportive exchange with you.

For a slightly older child who still cannot express himself well, you want to incorporate the sounds, gestures, and pattern recognition into playtime. Help him to relate patterns of words to a bigger picture than his immediate needs or favorite toys. His everyday life is expanding, so his playtime can too. For instance, certain games combine movement and word directions, such as the old standards Hide and Seek and Pin the Tail on the Donkey. (And of course, there is always Mother May I.) Playing the game will motivate the child to grasp the word patterns so he can ask the right questions and follow the instructions.

With Hide and Seek, one person hides, one person seeks, and another who knows where the hider is tells the seeker if he is hot or cold when he asks. He needs to do the asking; that is, he is motivated to do basic problem-solving. It's basically a precursor to a treasure hunt, which is another activity that combines all these elements. With Pin the Tail, you set it up as usual with the tail-less donkey picture and the blindfolded child holding the tail. You spin the child around, but instead of letting him grope about for the picture, he gets to ask you questions about what direction to take toward the picture. You give short, simple directions, such as two steps up, which he repeats and counts out (you can help with counting and hold his hand if needed) until he finds the picture. His goal is to pin the tail by asking questions; your goal is to motivate him to follow oral directions—to connect sound and movement. Whenever a game is a little too frustrating, try another game.

Through these games, children can practice problem-solving that incorporates words, patterns, and movement. The excitement of the game motivates him. He integrates his senses with emotion and expression so that the learning experience resonates more deeply, and he advances to a higher thinking level.

Building on Experience

Improving language skills begins with the steps we've just outlined: differentiate sounds, animate sounds, differentiate and animate blends, encourage words, and encourage sentences. One factor makes all this learning and practicing much easier. The most important element, which I want to stress again, is to engage the child by building on his existing interests and experiences, on what he already likes and feels comfortable with, on what he's involved with emotionally. That is, don't come at it from some arbitrary list or one sorted alphabetically but rather from the child's heart. This is critical because all learning starts with the child's emotional investment.

An emotional connection, a child's personal experience with a word or concept, not only motivates but also gives understanding. A child learns what an apple is not because you read him the dictionary definition but because he's tasted one, played with one, maybe even picked one from a tree. He has an opinion about an apple. A child learns what a mommy is because of all the experiences he has with his own: Mommy is warm and loving, Mommy says no, Mommy helps him. A child learns the words "Ma Ma" or "Da Da" because they are so full of meaning. We get to know a word by relating to what it represents to our senses and emotions in many different contexts in life, whether it's a telephone, a book, or a concept such as "liberty."

So to relate this idea directly to an example with sounds, let's say we have a child whose sounds or words (or phrases or sentences) are coming slowly. And let's say that every time he goes to the zoo, he darts for Monkey Island. He obviously likes monkeys, and even though he doesn't say the word, he has the concept in his head. Practicing this word is a natural. His parents can use a Socrates moment. At the zoo, if they point to the signpost with the arrow and the picture of the monkeys and ask him if he wants to see the monkeys or the lions (or whatever is on the signpost), he will understand and be very motivated to repeat the word monkey. Later, he can practice with pictures of monkeys in a book.

This little boy could have oral-motor problems that make the "muh" sound difficult for him. He might start by saying "uhnkey." He doesn't need to have a perfect sound match right away. Patient work on the "muh" sound will help. What's important is the concept that a series of sounds gets him something he wants. Once he gets the idea that he can let others know what he wants with one particular series of sounds, he's motivated to use symbolic language in general. So these first few excursions into language through experience-based words, phrases, and concepts open the door to a wider world of language.

I've worked with children who are slow to talk, and when I get them playing with something that's very emotionally meaningful to them, all of a sudden, their attempts at different sounds escalate. The key is to build on what children enjoy and care about, now and always. Then they are eager to try. An emotional connection gets their whole mental team working together rapidly.

Typically, the child with an auditory processing problem uses stronger processing areas to compensate for the weaker one. In the method we have described, we change this dynamic. First, we work on just the sounds, making sure the child has the basic foundation to make sounds, then we recruit the stronger sensory systems to help integrate the one that is a little weaker. We use vision; movement; and a lot of emotion, expression, and experience to make it easier for children to use and develop the listening part of their brain.

Here is a parallel example. Think of a muscle that is weak. Left alone, other muscles will compensate for it, keeping it from strengthening naturally. So first you have to isolate it and exercise it to feel it and get it going. Then you want to do exercises that let your developing muscle work in conjunction with your other muscles, so it becomes integrated and used in the total movement. The process is exactly the same for strengthening any sensory input that needs a boost.

Older children whose language development or reading is slow need to re-create this progression. For some reason, one of these steps might not be as solid as it should be. You need to create opportunities that pull in as many of the child's senses as possible to support the brain's efforts to differentiate sounds. That's where Floortime comes in, bringing everything together, so that the child's strengths—visual perception, movement, emotions—together bolster the auditory part at each level. And remember, the more challenging the task, the more fun it needs to be.

READING

After the above discussion, it won't surprise you that reading problems don't usually result from poor teaching or a lack of exposure to books. Children who have trouble reading often can't distinguish subtle sound differences. They have a "tin ear." The first skills that a child needs for strong language and reading skills are those we have just described—the abilities to decode sound, to hear and differentiate sounds along with their blends and patterns, and to understand how the sounds make up words. Without that foundation, there are no sound patterns to match to a visual image—a letter or word—on the page. Now suppose a child has the foundation but still has a problem.

Connecting Sounds to Visual Images

For kids who have decent language but still have trouble reading, I want them to get used to connecting sounds to images (the visual-sound system). To do this, I have them physically create their own shapes to represent a sound, a unique mini-alphabet. When asked, "How would you draw the 'duh' sound?" a child might make a loop, or for "kuh" an angle. He can use different colors if he wants. Then he can play a game to see if he can remember, reproduce, and maybe teach a parent the different squiggles he made for the "kuh" or "duh" or "muh." (This is part of the Lindamood-Bell approach mentioned above.)

At the beginning stage, anything goes—whatever his fine motor skills let him do, he should do, as long as there are unique images for the different sounds. Children begin to connect what they see (pictures they've made themselves so they're invested) with what they hear and say. The visual and motor systems support the sound system.

The next step for you as a parent is to explain another way of showing the "duh" sound. You print a "D" and have your child practice by tracing over it. Your child's fine motor system needs to be developed enough to do this. If not, you can help by putting your hand on top of his hand, or you can slowly print the letter and show it to him. Children with a delayed motor system can learn to read without printing clearly. If they use vision, emotions, movement, interaction, hearing, and speaking, they get many parts of the brain working together even if they can't form the letter well.

Children then move on to visually matching the sound of blends, "dr," "br," "qu," and so on, with the actual depiction, although blends are a little trickier. They're easier to learn as a blended sound rather than a combination of the individual sounds. As children master connecting sounds to visual images, they learn to sound out individual letters, blends, and eventually whole words.

You want to make your child see and do, not just listen and repeat; you want the learning experience to be alive and meaningful—in this case, an active mastery of the sounds that pulls all parts of the mind and brain together. The more actively involved he is, the quicker the child will master this or any other learning problem.

Word Comprehension

The next step is to help children comprehend the words they hear and read. A child may have a good ear and can repeat words back but doesn't really know what the words mean. He might be able to

sound out a long word such as "sympathetic" or he may have good
sight memory, but really to know what the word means and to understand it quickly in context, he has to have heard or used that
word in multiple contexts.

To support word comprehension, we again use two general principles: getting all the thinking parts working together and building
on interest and experience—whatever has meaning for the child,
monkeys in the zoo or trucks building a road. With a verbal child,
you two can read one of his favorite stories together and then talk
about it or make up a song that repeats the words in the story. Or he
can play out the action, taking the lead and directing the drama.
With a less verbal child, one who is still developing language and
can't read yet, you can read some of the text to him, look at the pictures together, exchange ideas using words from the story, and then
play it out. He will not be able to sound out the letters on the page,
but he will understand that they convey a story. A story lets him
expand his imagination to an exciting world that is waiting for him
when he learns to read. If the story is about a little dog who is lost, a
stuffed animal can take the starring role, or one of you can pretend
to be the dog and play out the drama together.

Here's the point—whatever a child's ability, he can dramatize
the story, using words in it and using his imagination. You and he
can even create a little storybook about something he's interested
in—writing sentences, finding pictures in magazines, or drawing
them—and then he can star in the production. He acts out the
words and context, broadening his usable vocabulary.

Some children can't quite translate pictures into drama. So you
give choices to help them understand context. If the picture in the
story shows a dog standing on the corner not knowing which way
to go and the child can't interpret the situation, you can offer,
"Well, should the little doggy cross the street, or should he wag his
tail because he's happy?" If the child makes a choice that doesn't
correspond to the text, you can say, "Oh, OK! Maybe the little dog

is happy because he sees a friend and wants to show it. So what does he do now?" Offer the child the same choice again, but switch the original sequence. (Remember the rule about getting your child to answer why questions: when you give your child choices to make him think, first give him the "correct" choice and second the incorrect or silly choice. This way he has to think and is less tempted to simply parrot back the last thing you say.)

This method for comprehension works down at the level of single words too. You can talk about what a new word means as well as act it out. For instance, perhaps your older child is studying marsupials, and you want to explain it to your littler one. You can show the child pictures of kangaroos and explain that marsupials carry their babies in a pouch. But if you give him an apron so that he can place a stuffed animal (a pretend joey) into the front pocket and hop around, he'll really understand and remember the concept. Or if the word is "weird," you can discuss things that are weird, and then let the child act weird. What weird expressions can he make? What weird hairstyles or clothes can he put together? When a child has fun and is personally involved with the word, the word will generalize immediately, becoming part of his emotional experience.

To recap, for word comprehension, whether written or spoken, whether simple like "truck" or more advanced like "authority," the best way for the child to understand and remember a word is by using things that are part of the child's daily world and letting him act it out, draw it, or make a story about it. Take advantage of whatever the child's interests are—sports, dance, music, or favorite toys. Use whatever is familiar and important to the child to help create meaning.

Memory and Words

Rather than getting confused because of problems processing the sounds, some children have a problem with memory—whether it is a series of letters or numbers. Children who can't repeat letters or numbers, backward or forward, have problems with auditory memory. They have difficulty remembering what they hear. If your child seems to have a memory problem, you can work on that by having him practice remembering things that he's interested in. For a boy who likes to trade baseball cards: "I'm going to tell you the names of these five [or four or whatever is a little stretch] players, and you can have as many as you can remember" is much better for improving memory than "Recite back to me the following letters or numbers."

PRACTICING

Just because you've helped your child to understand that sounds make up words, to learn the alphabet, and to identify printed letters does not mean he will become a natural reader overnight. At some point he needs to practice. And for a seven-year-old sitting there holding a whole book (even if it's only twenty pages), the task can feel daunting. (Think about reading a book in a foreign language that you don't know well and how difficult that would be.) Making reading a special time and giving a little help can be a big boost. All it takes is a special partner. You or another special person in his life can listen enthusiastically, maybe even adding in sound effects. If he reads a story about a dog, he can tell you when to do the "Arf, arf"s.

Or you can share the reading. A struggling reader can get pretty tired out, so you can give him a short breather by reading every other page. He will keep practicing longer and not develop such a feeling of burden. Ask him if there is something special that you can do to make it more fun for him. If he doesn't know, suggest a few things and let him choose. And of course the book should also be his to choose, following his favorite subject.

An environment that nurtures a child's first reading adventures uses all the senses in an emotionally meaningful way, starts with words familiar to the child, and lets a child feel a sense of mastery. The excitement in the child will build when he has a solid foundation—when he has listened to a sound and imitated it, then connected the sound to its image, both visually and with movement (writing it in the air or on paper or walking it out on the floor). Some children will do these steps with relative ease and don't need all of them. They will recognize and say words that you don't specifically teach them. Some children will seem to do well with the words you teach them but won't be able to sound out easy new words. They may be using visual memory, in which case you want to go through the basic steps for sounding out words.

How well does your child decipher sounds?

A. When your child hears new words, he . . .

1. Often struggles to reproduce them
2. Is unable to reproduce those with many syllables or foreign words
3. Keeps trying until he gets it
4. Enjoys learning new words, even if they are complicated

B. When playing a game of matching up letters and blends with their sounds, your child . . .

1. Gets easily confused with which sound goes to which letter or blend
2. Gets confused by certain letters and sounds
3. Can match the correct sound to the letter but takes awhile
4. Matches the sounds and the letters easily

continues

continued

C. If you give your child a string of directions, he . . .

1. Routinely gets lost in the process and doesn't complete the task
2. Can follow a simple, two-step set of directions but otherwise gets lost
3. Can follow a more complex, multistep set of directions with some uncertainty
4. Can follow complex directions and improvise, if need be, to get the desired outcome

D. When your child has a new experience—for instance, sees a fortress with a moat for the first time and learns the word "moat"—he . . .

1. Never uses the new word when relating the experience to friends
2. Mentions the new detail but doesn't use the new word to describe it
3. Mentions the new detail and, the first time or two, struggles to use the new word
4. Enjoys using the new word in the correct way

Marilyn Nolt

Making Sense of What We Hear

The last chapter explained how deciphering sounds is the foundation for developing language, learning to read, and comprehending what you read. By refining auditory processing at the higher levels of thinking, children strengthen their verbal ability and improve their powers of abstract thinking. They become able to construct and explain larger conceptual pictures.

This chapter gives selected examples of reading problems for children at higher thinking levels. The first example shows how an older child can coordinate auditory processing with other senses. The second addresses children who have problems with understanding instructions. And the third looks at verbal abstracting skills and how they can be improved by involving personal experience.

How does a child learn to integrate information from sounds with information from other parts of the central nervous system—such as visual processing and motor functioning—at the higher thinking levels? With older children, the problems are a little tougher, but the approach is basically the same as in the previous chapter—exercises that connect multiple senses at once.

INTEGRATING AUDITORY PROCESSING
WITH THE OTHER SENSES: ISABELLE

Isabelle, a sixteen-year-old, didn't have a straightforward problem with reading or auditory processing. But she did need help. A gifted singer, she struggled to sight-read music, a serious drawback because she wanted to be a professional singer. Her teachers had never identified a problem with her regular reading ability—she was a top student—but in fact she didn't particularly enjoy reading books. When she did read, she had to pay close attention to dig out the information. Abstract thinking, though, wasn't a basic issue because when she heard it, rather than read it, she understood. The same with music. Hearing a complex musical composition and repeating it was easy. She had a good ear. Her auditory processing was just fine.

Isabelle decided to get some help with sight-reading and went to see Harry Wachs, author of *Thinking Goes to School* and an expert in visual-spatial processing and thinking. He saw that Isabelle's problem centered on connecting what she was seeing (the musical notes) with what she was hearing (her voice) and converting one to the other. The problem wasn't with higher levels of verbal abstraction or with her ear, her memory, or her vision. It was with conversion—what she saw into what she heard.

Basically, Isabelle's problem was just a more sophisticated version of one we saw in the last chapter, with young children who needed to create their own visual images of sounds—their own alphabet—to connect a sound with a written representation. Isabelle was well past the basic links. It was the more complex ones that tripped her up. She had to strengthen not only those in the visual-sound systems but also those in the visual-motor systems to create an ability that she could rely on. The motor system is important because producing sounds requires coordination of the muscles in the head, throat, chest, and diaphragm. That's what she started working on first.

Visual-Motor Connections

Isabelle's initial set of exercises to tackle the visual-motor connection was the most fundamental: familiar hand/foot–eye exercises, such as catching or kicking balls. She coordinated her vision with movement at a very basic level. Moving on to a slightly more advanced exercise, she watched small lights on a board flash a certain pattern that changed randomly. She had to respond by touching a button as quickly as possible when she saw the pattern change. This exercise helped to develop her tracking ability.

Another visual-motor exercise Isabelle worked on used colors as visual codes that indicate specific actions. Red means one step left; pink means two steps left; bright green means one step forward; forest green means two steps forward, and so on for the left and backward (or diagonal to be really fancy). A helper held up a colored square of paper, and Isabelle responded with the corresponding move. Showing the different colors more quickly increased the complexity. (Flashing light patterns to indicate different directions create the same game.)

Visual-Sound Connections

Next, Isabelle performed exercises to connect visual images with sounds. She would hear a letter, such as "A" or "B," and as letters lit up randomly on a board, she would press a button when the letter was highlighted. The exercise directly connected her strong auditory ability to her weaker visual ability. After quickly mastering this task, she faced a more complicated one: to hear a letter, for instance "B," transpose it to the next higher letter in the alphabet, "C," and then find that letter on the board. This game has many levels of difficulty, such as hearing a letter and then transposing to a lower letter or transposing to a letter that is two higher or lower. The speed of lighting up of the letters increases difficulty.

Sound-Motor Connections

Isabelle had one more combination to master—sound and motor connections. As with the game above where colors represented a directional code, letters or numbers can also be codes. It starts with creating the code—the letter code "A" means "move right," "B" means "move left," "C" means "move forward," "D" means "move backward," and so forth. The letters or numbers are then spoken so that the auditory system is exercised. When letters were called out, Isabelle followed the coded instructions. Hearing three or four letters in a row made it more difficult.

Using number or letter codes to signify directions can also create a variation on a treasure hunt. This added aspect may increase the interest of a younger child and let other children join in more readily. If several children compete to reach the treasure, the action automatically quickens.

Visual-Motor-Sound Connections

The last challenge for Isabelle was to connect all three systems— vision, sound, and motion—at once. Here is one example. A code is created that combines a spoken letter with a visual color to create directions, where "A" plus green equals "left," "B" plus red equals "right," and so on. The helper calls out a letter and holds up a color while the participant makes the correct move after converting the letter-color code into the corresponding instruction.

Alternatively, the combination codes (letters/colors) can be instructions to kick your leg, swing your arms, turn your head, or whatever movement you want. Only imagination limits variations on these exercises. The key is to set the first challenge so that the child can reach a certain success rate, that is, not to make it so tough that the child gets discouraged. Most children, if they can achieve a 70–80 percent success rate, are motivated to go on. Of course, the faster the codes are given out, or the more that are given out in one interval, the more difficult the exercise. The task can be made harder in small increments.

Isabelle's Music Sight-Reading

After all these exercises that strengthened the connections between her senses, Isabelle was ready to tackle sight-reading music again. By chance, her music teacher used an approach developed by Swiss musician Émile-Jaques Dalcroze some 100 years ago, an approach similar to our philosophy of the Learning Tree. That is, he emphasized incorporating movement, sight, sound, and emotion to strengthen sight-reading. Isabelle was ready. Through physically expressing a phrase of music, interacting with others, and visualizing the composition in space, Isabelle then successfully learned to integrate such aspects of music as pitch, scale, note values, rhythm, and the quality of the sound. Not an easy task for anyone, but for Isabelle it was a huge accomplishment, one that shows the power of determination as well as the importance of using strengths to boost weaknesses.

UNDERSTANDING AND FOLLOWING INSTRUCTIONS: JACK

Teens can have language processing problems for a host of reasons. Some have overcome more pervasive developmental problems (perhaps being diagnosed on the autistic spectrum) and are left with a language problem. Others are slow to talk and go on to have a hard time learning to read, a problem we discussed in the previous chapter. There are still others who show no signs of a language problem in the early grades, but when they get to high school, they have trouble writing essays or answering exam questions because they misread the question or directions. The increased complexity of high school work can let problems emerge for the first time.

One such child, whom I'll call Jack, was having trouble answering certain essay questions on exams. When the question was straightforward, such as, "What were the causes of the Revolutionary War? Discuss," Jack would do well. He was a good abstract thinker, and he could organize his response well and elaborate on it. His difficulty arose with complex questions: "Scholars have written about many causes of the Revolutionary War. Some of these causes have not been substantiated and, therefore, should no longer be given credence. Others are more relevant to the modern context for war than the Revolutionary War. Discuss your view of the causes of the Revolutionary War in relationship to the above qualifying statements." When it came to a convoluted, multipart question, Jack got lost, even though the question was essentially the same as the uncomplicated one. An anxious and disorganized Jack would write about wars in Iraq and Vietnam and make some fragmented references to the Revolutionary War.

Jack, who was fifteen, had a lot of potential. He was a warm, friendly guy who had a fairly good intuitive sense about people and relationships. He got As and Bs in science and math and did well in the straightforward parts of English. Yet in class discussions and even in conversation with friends, Jack could come across as "not getting it." If a conversation were subtle or involved complex verbal interchanges, he would often get confused and say to himself, "What did that person actually mean?" That same confusion pervaded his schoolwork when it involved answering these complex, multipart questions in history or English. He would usually fall on his face and get a D or even an F.

Sequencing

There are large numbers of older children with this type of auditory processing problem. (Remember Anna, who couldn't fetch her shoes? She had this problem at a more primary thinking level. And our friend Sally in the first chapter had it with reading.) They receive various diagnoses—from "central auditory processing disorder" to "pragmatic language disorder" to "dyslexia." But the central problem, whether involving reading comprehension, essay writing, or verbal exchanges, is with the ability to hold in mind multiple pieces of related verbal information and complex sequences. Perhaps someone says: "Well, you know, you're a nice person and lots of fun, and I like you but not when you do [such and such]. Sometimes when you do [such and such], it reminds me of my sister when she used to do [this or that], and I think that's why it bothers me." The child who can't keep all that in mind has no idea where she stands with the other person. She can't hold the first statement in mind long enough for the speaker to get to a qualifying statement, which may be the third or fourth item in the sequence. (Think back to the discussion about attention deficit disorder and the example of trying to understand a long set of road directions from a person with an accent.)

This may seem like a purely auditory memory problem (such as discussed in the last chapter), but it's not because in addition to holding little bits of information in your memory, you need to understand the meaning of each part. Here's the difference. Suppose you are trying to memorize the words to a song that is in a language you don't speak versus a song in your own language. Without understanding the meaning of the words, you have nothing to help you hold the words in place except your memory. Basically you memorize nonsense words. That is a straight use of pure memory. But with a song in your own language, you use the meaning to help bring the words to mind and keep them in the proper sequence. Learning that native-language song involves both memory and meaning.

So, the problem in following complex instructions reduces to abstracting meanings very quickly, holding in mind those meanings and sequences, and seeing them juxtaposed with one another. Sequencing is a function of both memory and abstract meanings. For some children, memory could be a piece of their problem, but in Jack's case, that wasn't so.

Sequencing problems can arise in various academic subject areas, and often they are not present across the board. It is very common for children who can sequence well in math and science to be weaker at it in areas requiring verbal skills, such as English or history (that was Jack's pattern), and vice versa for those who can easily sequence verbal instructions but can't do it with mathematical symbols. Because of the "not getting it" factor, sequencing affects social relationships too—altering children's social skills and their confidence in themselves.

The question then is, What kind of practice would help Jack?

Please hold this question in mind for a minute. Let's take a quick diversion to describe different kinds of memory problems just to put this issue to rest.

Memory Difficulties

As with the diagnoses of learning problems noted in the introductory chapter to the roots, memory problems get diagnosed frequently. Various terms—"recent memory," "working memory," and "declarative memory"—are used to talk about them. But often they are symptoms of something else. Definitions help explain why.

"Recent memory" relates to events that happened in the last few hours or days. The elderly in the early stages of Alzheimer's or those who have cerebral vascular disease will lose recent memory. But it's unusual to see these problems in children, other than in those with some kind of metabolic or progressive neurological disorder. If you ask a child to explain to you the rules for Capture the Flag and she can't answer, there are many possible reasons. For instance, she didn't listen to your question; she understood your question but can't sequence the rules well enough to form an answer; she understood and listened but was fooling around with friends while playing and didn't pay attention to the rules; or she has a neurological disorder (the least likely).

"Working memory" usually refers to memory that we use to solve a problem in the here and now: how to play a computer game or how to get lunch. A child using her working memory takes elements from recent memory and from history—things she's done before—and uses them to solve the problem. Children diagnosed with working memory problems often have trouble synthesizing the different parts of their sensory system with their thinking levels. What appears to be a working memory problem may be a problem with overreacting to sensation, which disrupts the child's ability to attend to the task at hand. Or it may be a problem with understanding the visual pattern or with planning or sequencing the actions. Again, we have to break down the child's actual difficulty. (Other types of memory, such as "declarative memory," which refers to our conscious memory; "episodic memory," which refers to specific events that we've experienced; and "nonconscious memory," which refers to skills we acquire that are part of our makeup, are not usually associated with learning disabilities.)

We certainly want to pay attention to memory problems, but it's important to look at the contributing roots and make sure that a possible memory problem is not covering up something more basic.

Here is an irony. Sometimes children have such good memories that in the early grades they slide by on them and don't develop an understanding of the concepts. In fact, they don't really know that they don't understand the material because they can recite it to you. When the concepts become more abstract, maybe around fourth or fifth grade, and memory alone isn't enough, learning disabilities can show up seemingly out of the blue. On the other hand, kids who have to work to understand at an early age because they don't have great memories sometimes develop a deeper insight into the concepts so that they can keep them in mind. As the concepts become more abstract, the analytic abilities that their poor memories made them nurture support their learning. They often flourish in college, to the surprise of many. There is more than one Nobel prize–winning physicist with a poor memory who struggled in the early grades because of the rote teaching method but compensated by developing strong abstract thinking skills.

Going back to Jack (who didn't have a memory problem), let's see what he can do about those problems that he did have.

Sequencing Practice

Jack's parents had already hired a tutor. I recommended to his tutor that Jack get more practice in the problem area—interpreting complex verbal and written information. The tutor said, "He's getting plenty of practice. He's assigned at least one essay a week." I pointed out that was just once a week and that the problem wasn't in writing an essay but in interpreting the question. Because the tutor saw Jack for one and a half hours twice a week, Jack could be given ten questions to read and interpret per session, making for twenty practice opportunities each week, not just one.

His tutor agreed to give Jack plenty of questions to interpret, and Jack's teachers contributed their old exams and essay assignments to the effort. Jack started off simply by analyzing two-segment questions and expanded to two segments with one negative statement. As they became ever more complex, he eventually got to a four-part question: "What did the generals who were considered to be the best and the generals who were considered to have made the biggest blunders see as the strengths and weaknesses in the conduct of the Revolutionary War? How did the best and the worst generals in the Civil War assess the conduct of that war? Are there any similarities between the opinions of the best and the worst generals in the two wars?" This was a multipart question that required holding a lot of information in mind—just the kind of question that gave Jack a headache.

Practice at Home

Support on the home front was important too. During conversations, his parents began making their comments and questions a little more complicated. They would say "That's good when you do [X] but not you when do [Y]" kind of statements. Or "Gee, I noticed that you played really hard in soccer practice today. Does that mean you are starting to like soccer as well as basketball?"

Noticing that Jack sometimes lost the thread of conversations, his parents had unconsciously decreased the complexity of their conversation with him. Now they spoke at their own adult level, making observations and asking questions that made him practice thinking at the comparative and gray-area level—first, simple comparisons, and then, relative differences between things. His parents allowed the discussion to become gradually more complex so that over time Jack had to hold more and more complex information in mind, to remember what they were saying, and to interpret the meaning quickly. As we saw, simple memorization wasn't a problem for Jack; rather, it was the rapid interpretation of many abstract verbal meanings in a row—and I emphasize the words "many" and "rapid." If something was abstract in a straightforward way, he could think through at the lower multicausal level. For the question, "Why do you think Mark Twain created the character of Huck Finn?" Jack wrote an elegant essay giving many reasons to support his idea that Huck Finn, with his adventurous spirit, was really the boy Mark Twain wished he could have been. On the output side he was a sophisticated, verbal thinker, just not on the input side.

Potential

Sometimes one hurdle gets blown into a whole obstacle course. This is especially true for children who are slow at following instructions or answering complex questions. Some people might say of Jack, "Well, he's just not a very smart kid," or, "He's okay in math and science, but he's never going to win any writing awards." But by identifying and correcting the right problem, Jack could write books, do math and science, or do both. By getting over this one hurdle, he'd have his choice.

Children are often smarter than we give them credit for, but they do vary in terms of their processing capacities. They can be uneven in their central nervous system development. Time, however, is on their side. There's no horse race here. They don't have to be at their peak when they're thirteen or fourteen, or even equal to other kids by their junior year of high school. That's why some kids who just plugged along in high school shine in college—the so-called "late bloomers." What happens is that, along with their growth and development and some help, they finally get enough practice to get over some of these glitches and hurdles.

Rather than see problems as global, the idea is to figure out where the problem exists. It's easy to say that a child doesn't understand subtleties or isn't terribly reflective. Factual though these characterizations may be, they often may be too general to be useful in correcting the problem. Consider our discussion about ADHD in the introductory chapter to the roots. There can be multiple causes. Without figuring out which one it is, the recourse is to treat the symptom only. The underlying problem never gets addressed and resolved. One underlying hurdle keeps blocking the way and complicating the whole picture. With auditory problems, as well as with the rest of the roots, we need to pinpoint the exact difficulty. Is it in understanding certain words and concepts and, if so, what's the reason? Is it because the child can sequence two or three words in a row but not five or six, or two clauses but not four? Is it that the child hasn't been exposed to a subject in a personal, meaningful way? This last question relates to a child we will call Eric.

UNDERSTANDING ABSTRACT CONCEPTS VIA
PERSONAL EXPERIENCES: ERIC AND CLAIRE

Eric, like Jack, had a problem with higher levels of language comprehension—obvious from his jumbled essay answers. But Eric's problem was different. Rather than not being able to sequence, he couldn't relate to the topic.

In the last chapter, we discussed using children's interests and emotions as threads to pull them into engaging and strengthening their auditory system. Children's own interests will entice them to organize and expand their vocabulary and, eventually, concepts. Conversely, children with limited experiences sometimes can't quite grasp a particular concept or relate a specific experience to a similar one in a different context. In this way, an incomprehensible essay question on a subject unfamiliar to the child becomes a confused essay answer.

Eric's teacher (another Mark Twain fan) assigned an essay about the competition between Huck Finn and his father. Eric was at a loss, as was often the case, and so were his parents after seeing the same problem with essays come up for Eric over and over again. They brought him to see me.

When a child seems confused about an academic exercise, the first thing to check is whether he actually grasps the question. (A problem for both Eric and Jack but, as explained, for different reasons.) I asked him, "Do you understand what the words 'competition' and 'rivalry' mean?" and he shook his head, saying, "Well, kind of. I know that you can have a competition in a game, but what does that have to do with Huck and his father? They aren't playing a game." Eric couldn't relate.

Certainly in higher grades, but even in Eric's seventh-grade class, children don't usually have free choice of essay topics. So, if they have trouble relating to questions, they need to discover how to gain an emotional, experiential connection to it. To help Eric see a connection, I used the time-tested strategy of linking the topic to the familiar experience of family relationships, the universal common denominator. Family relationships are tailor-made for exploring emotional connections and are my staple for these kinds of problems. It's a simple tactic as well for parents to use because they can quickly hone in on a family dynamic that relates to the essay question at hand. Importantly, to make the link, the child also needs comparative and gray-area thinking skills. She needs to be able to compare her experiences with someone else's.

I said to Eric, "You have a brother, right? What happens when you both want to play with the Nintendo DS?" Eric described their arguing and fighting, after which I asked, "So, who wins?"

"Well," he said, "I do most of the time. I'm bigger."

"Eric," I explained, "You and your brother 'compete' for the Nintendo DS. That's called a 'competition.' Now, do you think you ever compete with your father over something?"

He said, "Yeah, sometimes I want to kick the ball around, and my dad wants to shoot hoops. He says I throw a fit until I get my way." Thoughtfully, he continued, "I guess I win then too." Through an emotional situation that was personally relevant, Eric broadened his concept of competition.

So I said, "In that section of the book where Huck's father tries to keep him locked in a cabin and Huck wants out, what's happening with the competition?"

"Hmmm," Eric replied, "Huck doesn't want to stay and figures out how to outsmart his father. He sneaks around and goes off with his friend, even though his father tells him not to. So he actually wins." Once Eric had a more general idea of competition, it was easy to lead him to connect the more abstract material about Huck Finn and his father. He thought at the comparative level.

Some children can naturally relate abstract situations to their personal experiences; others need coaching. Once children can make comparisons relating to their friends and family and can dismantle complex questions about these, they can begin applying the same analytical principles to literary figures, current events, or topics of less intrinsic interest. Fumbling this initial connection doesn't indicate a fundamental language deficit. If the basics are strong, children can use their experiences to deepen the higher levels of verbal abilities and abstract thinking to improve comprehension.

Fourteen-year-old Claire had a problem that required a similar approach to Eric's. Her problem: analyzing novels. She couldn't see the themes, and she didn't really understand the characters and the complexity of the relationships. This is an issue of sequencing—in this case, Claire had a difficult time pulling together what she heard or read into a big picture. To reach this level, children need to address the question, "How does all this work together?" As with Eric, when kids use their own experiences, it leads to a solution because it helps them to see the big picture and at the same time brings them to the highest thinking level, reflective thinking.

Once again, family relationship patterns are useful. For Claire, this meant her sisters Melissa and Amy as well as Mom and Dad. There were things family members did that Claire liked and things that she didn't like. A question that arises is, What do all these people have in common? Or, what's the big picture? Answering this question requires extracting the common features, thinking reflectively. This is not to turn children into junior mental health professionals. But because they usually like to chat about their family, a good questioner and listener can spark a child's emotional insights and help to make connections—that is, practice sequencing at the reflective level of thinking.

The topic could just as easily be Claire's favorite singers, authors, or friends at school if these are more comfortable for her to talk about. The point is to look for common themes and to strengthen the ability for self-reflection—so that Claire can say things like, "My sister Melissa is different from me because she tries to be the goody-two-shoes with my parents, and I like to be my own person."

When children can think reflectively about personal topics, they can soon branch out to use reflective and abstract thinking to improve their reading comprehension—for instance, as in Claire's case, to understand the motives of a character in a novel. This is because abstract thinking means using one's personal perspective for insight and then adapting those insights to a different, abstract context. It doesn't mean having an experience and assuming that everyone else would have the same reaction. People who do that personalize everything; they get lost in their own perspective.

True abstract thinking is being able to say, "If that happened to me, how would I feel? I'd feel angry. But she's different. She likes to do things for other people. She might feel sorry for the person who was mean to her." By practicing to understand her own feelings and to abstract across characteristics, Claire can learn to go back and forth between the personal and the abstract: "How is the person in the novel similar to me, and how is she different? What social pressures does she feel, and what would I feel? How would these differences lead to different responses or a different understanding of the situation?" This way, we use insight about ourselves and others to generate a truly abstract perspective.

Reflection means having a sense of who you are and being able to compare other experiences to your own in a logical and realistic manner. In this way, children bring meaning to what they hear and read and move from understanding simple sounds to grasping a sequence of abstract ideas.

We have not included questions for this chapter or for Chapter 11 because the examples with school-age children let you relate them directly to your child.

10

Organizing Actions
Motor Planning and Sequencing

We all recognize them. The kid who gets chosen last for the sports team. Or the one everyone else hopes doesn't show up to play in the big game. The kids who can't learn to ride a bike, and the kids who make excuses not to go to gym class. They hedge to cover up their self-consciousness and embarrassment, but a parent's eye sees it immediately. If it is your child, you feel a pang and worry: is he just naturally clumsy and destined to be the brunt of locker room jokes? It is a tough question to confront, but, fortunately, the answer is no.

More than likely, the child's lack of grace and coordination comes from a problem with motor planning and sequencing. But problems in this area don't stop at athletic ability. These terms relate to how we create an action plan to solve a problem and then execute the action—that is, how we organize our facial muscles to give a nuanced expression, how we adjust our vocal tone to make it assertive but not aggressive, how we playfully and gently push a friend and not accidentally hurt him, or how we efficiently follow the teacher's instructions for getting ready to take a test or copy down information from the board. (Complex analysis of these actions leads to a breakdown into many subfactors. We are using motor planning and sequencing as the broad category.)

Motor planning and sequencing is not only a factor in our athletic success but also one in our success at school, with friends, and in everyday functioning. As I mentioned earlier, almost all the children I see who get diagnosed with ADHD or ADD have problems with planning and sequencing. If a child gets lost on the way to the bathroom because he can't plan four actions in a row, he not only seems inattentive—he *is* inattentive. But it's because he can't sequence actions easily; he can't keep the steps of an action plan in mind. Of course, there is always the exception of the clumsy kid who is a whiz at business plans (or the absent-minded professor we mentioned a few chapters back) and the super-athlete who can't plan anything complex. But most people who can plan and sequence motor actions can plan and sequence thoughts and emotions too.

So imagine being a child who can't plan and sequence his actions. He wants to catch that ball—but he doesn't quite get his hands together in time, and it goes right through his fingers. He tries so hard—but there is seemingly a hole in his hands. He tries to write down the math problems on the board and is only half finished when the teacher goes on to the next subject. Perhaps a girl wants to skip rope at recess with the other girls—but she barely gets through "Down in the valley where the green grass grows," let alone gets a kiss, before the rope trips her up.

This chapter focuses on exercises to improve children's gross motor planning with some discussion of fine motor planning too. Whether kids have low muscle tone, poor balance or coordination, or problems with left/right integration or hand-eye coordination, they can improve with these exercises. Interacting with a parent or caregiver lets them practice creating action plans and implementing them. The continuous back-and-forth of the exercises helps basic movements become rhythmic and coordinated and, eventually, automatic. These abilities will usually lead to improved planning and sequencing in all areas as they mature.

THE STAGES OF
MOTOR PLANNING AND SEQUENCING

Attention and Engaging the World

To understand how motor planning and sequencing develop, we start really far back—the unborn baby. As an unborn baby's nervous system matures, particularly the cerebellum and the frontal lobes, his random movements slowly become more rhythmic and synchronous, not just from reactions to internal sensations but to outside ones too. A little rub on the tummy from Mom or the lilt of a nighttime lullaby can start baby turning or kicking in a particular pattern. With newborns, we see this even more clearly: rhythmic movements in reaction to Mommy's voice and other sounds.

This rhythmicity is the beginning of motor organization and a primary piece of motor planning and sequencing. Babies who have delays in the development of their nervous system—because of oxygen-loss at birth or some other biological challenge—often have a delay in forming this synchrony and engagement with the world. Their movements are more random. As they grow, their rhythm and timing continue to be less rather than more predictable.

As rhythmic motion progresses from instinctual to purposeful, the driving factor is emotion. The baby turns toward his mother's voice because he finds it soothing and pleasurable. The reward of finding his mother's face makes him want to repeat the action. When he is able to follow her face, he gets the best reward—a big smile. Engagement, emotion, motor planning, and sequencing all work together.

The growing emotional connection creates a need, which, in turn, leads to the purposeful, organized action. A baby's reaction to a parent is what we call a "SAM"—a sensory affect motor response, rather than just a sensory motor action. The affect—in other words, emotion—determines the planned action. If the baby finds Mother's voice aversive (perhaps because he is sensitive to certain sounds), he may not attend and look toward her but instead reflexively look away or even act startled.

Interaction and Communication

Single-step, purposeful actions gradually expand into four- or five-step ones. By nine months of age, babies can look at Mommy's face, reach for the colorful ball she is holding, take the ball, examine it, hand it back to her, and then—if Mommy hides the ball in her hand—search for its hiding place. These are purposeful, sequential, flowing actions that respond to the mother's actions and fulfill an emotional need. The baby is communicating through reciprocal actions, as in playful, giggly games of Peek-a-Boo.

This stage, sustaining long, back-and-forth gesturing, is significant. Many children with dyspraxia—the formal term for problems with planning and completing motor tasks—tune out at this stage because they can't organize purposeful reactions. Parents of children with these problems may remember difficulties at this stage. If children can't get into a rhythm with another person, they don't get pulled into a strong relationship. I would estimate that at least 50 percent of children with moderate to severe motor planning problems are not good at such continuous communication. Later, these children may be given the label of "inattentive" or that of ADHD/ADD. The problem may have started at this point, when these motor planning or sensory difficulties interfered with their being drawn into an engaging, focused relationship. One sees this most profoundly with children who are on the autistic spectrum. They repeat the same one- or two-step actions—such as putting toy cars in a row—because they can't plan more complicated sequences or establish more personal connections.

Shared Problem-Solving

In the second year, children begin to initiate actions to get what they want. Babbled words, at least single ones, along with actions and gestures—pointing, showing, smiling—are all used to further a toddler's desires. By the time they are eighteen months old, they can search for a hidden toy that makes a noise. This shows their motor planning and sequencing as well as visual-spatial skills.

Here's a child putting these skills to work in a grocery store:

> Mom is pushing a cart down the produce aisle with sixteen-month-old Jennie, an avid scrutinizer of Mom's choices, perched in the cart seat. Jennie sees the bananas, pulls on Mom's hand pushing the cart, points and strains toward the fruit, while mouthing "ba." Her eager expression flashes "Gimme." Smiling and nodding in rhythm, Mom asks, "Jennie, should we buy some bananas?" To sounds of "ba, ba," Mom picks up a bunch of bananas and says, "How about these?" Getting a big smile in response, she holds the bananas momentarily close to her daughter so Jennie can touch them and fully enjoy her success. Jennie is elated that her own actions solved her problem. And Mom has closed the circle.

Their multistep communication combines in an orderly, connected (rather than free-associative or random) sequence and clearly addresses a problem—Jennie's desire for bananas.

This scenario reveals another factor—the quality of the reaction. When you need someone's help in solving a problem, you watch for that person's response. Whatever response you receive, anything from pleasure to surprise to irritability, affects how you plan your next step. So, unless the other person is unusually consistent, you are constantly challenged to create a new approach. This is why there is a different quality to the activity between a child and a caregiver and the quality of activity for a child who plays a pop-up game on his own. The latter is more likely to lapse into repetitive play. Although the child may move in a rhythm as he hits the pop-up piece, he has no need to create a new action plan after each reaction.

Emotional responses guide purposeful actions. A child's pleasurable connection to his partner drives his interest, involvement, persistence, and solution to problems. Thus to strengthen motor planning abilities, a child needs a partner who is emotionally invested. It could be a parent, a babysitter, a teacher, or another caregiver. Children improve motor planning skills by interacting with other people.

TYPES OF MOTOR PLANNING PROBLEMS

Children can experience motor problems at any point because their nervous system is continually becoming more complex, and the need for more elaborate coordination and sequencing becomes greater. For instance, between the ages of ten and twelve months, children gain more organized integration of the left and right sides of their bodies. The prefrontal cortex, which develops around that same time, helps coordinate the two hemispheres of the brain: the left side, which controls the right side of the body, and the right side, which controls the left side of the body. To achieve higher levels of motor planning and sequencing, we need both sides of the brain working together. Many children with motor planning and motor sequencing problems (or as the next chapter describes, problems with sequencing ideas) have trouble with left/right integration. Movement, especially movement that crosses over the midline of the body, stimulates the brain and the connections between both hemispheres.

Children with low muscle tone and relative weakness have another type of problem. They may have a mild form of cerebral palsy or some other problem that was not apparent in early development. They need to strengthen muscles so as to implement the actions they plan.

In other children, motor planning and sequencing problems are compounded when they get overloaded or overwhelmed by sensations. They can neither limit the amount of sensory input nor discharge this overload effectively because of their poor motor planning. Helplessness and anxiety often result, as we describe in Chapter 12.

Occupational and physical therapists as well as pediatric neurologists and physical medicine specialists can help design a program for children with left/right asymmetry, low muscle tone, or sensory-motor challenges. A general principle for consulting a specialist is to do so when the child's problem creates a negative impact on an important area of his life—making friends, doing well in school, feeling good in his family, or feeling good about himself. A consultation can help you understand the full nature of the problem and let you receive guidance from a professional experienced with such problems. The following exercises are helpful in a general sense. If you decide to work with a therapist as well, they can supplement the specialist's recommendations.

EXERCISES TO IMPROVE MOTOR PLANNING AND SEQUENCING

Motor control makes motor planning possible. The exercises below focus on strengthening muscles as well as on strengthening the connection between muscles and motor planning and sequencing.

These games and exercises help the child move through the first stages of motor planning and sequencing just discussed: engagement, rhythmic communication, interaction, and problem-solving. If your child is older or more verbal, the next chapter provides examples for the higher levels of sequencing.

Exercises are only as helpful as a child's interest in them. If you're enthusiastic, your child will probably like the ones described here. But if he doesn't, come up with something that he both enjoys and, like the Evolution Game below, that involves all the large muscle groups, coordination, balance, left/right integration, muscle tone, and rhythm.

The Evolution Game starts with the simple and progresses to the complex, both overall and within each "evolutionary" stage. You'll know when to advance to the next stage or a more difficult exercise within the stage by watching your child's proficiency. Start off with an exercise that your child can do decently and gradually increase the complexity so that your child maintains a high success rate. Success motivates children to keep trying, as does adding in competition with you where the child wins 70–80 percent of the time. You can level the playing field by either giving your child an advantage or handicapping yourself. You can add diversity and creativity by pulling in other senses, especially sound. Basically, you want to come up with increasingly complicated movements that involve a lot of interaction.

For older children or teenagers who might consider the Evolution Game too babyish, you can help build motor planning and sequencing skills with the balance and coordination activities described below.

The Evolution Game

The first primordial rung on the evolutionary ladder is the lowly but highly organized worm. Question: how does a worm wiggle forward?

Not with hands, feet, elbows, or toes. All they have is a long tummy. So, you and your child can try it together. As you twist, wiggle, squirm, and jiggle, you mimic a piece of the evolution of human movement.

Start the game off by getting down on the floor and wiggling like a worm (or snake, if you wish), just rocking back and forth, getting the body moving, trying to move from one place to another. It's not easy—and highlights the need for rhythmic movement. (You might turn on some music to promote rhythm.) You want to really engage your trunk muscles to copy the action patterns of a wiggly worm. This gives the central core a good workout, which is very helpful for children with low muscle tone or coordination difficulties. Practice the motion until your child can do it with some ease. To increase the complexity, try wiggling in synchrony. First, one of you sets the pace, and then the other does. Try to maintain a continuous rhythm. (Tip: put a sheet of plastic on the floor to make wiggling easier. Make sure to cover your skin so that it doesn't stick or get irritated.)

Your next stop up the evolutionary ladder is the lazy alligator or crocodile stage. You go from wiggling to modified slithering, not really up on all fours yet—just pushing a little with your toes/feet and elbows. If your child is having trouble with this motion, put your hands behind his feet so that he can push off to start moving across the floor. A special treat on the other side of the room— something the child wants—adds incentive and a positive feeling when achieved—as does racing you when the child gets to win.

This rung on the ladder, as well as the others, also lends itself to strengthening a child's thinking. It begins, of course, with engaging the child. If your child is verbal, make up a story together. Does he want to be an alligator or a crocodile? How about the crocodile's name or personality? Why does the crocodile need to get across the room? After the game, you can find out what he liked and disliked about it. This will prompt him to reflect, to connect ideas together, and to help him examine and explain his feelings. If your child is one of those who has low muscle tone but has reached a higher thinking level, you'll get multiple ideas about why he liked it or didn't and even get some gray-area thinking that compares this game to others that you play. Just crossing the room, your slithering alligator can have elaborate, creative, and logical discussions, using many different thinking levels and strengthening the tree trunk while executing action plans and improving muscle tone.

Four-legged animals (whom we mimic by crawling on our hands and knees) are your next rung. You and your child get to imitate your child's favorite—playful dogs, cats, mice, horses, whatever he likes. Crawling games not only use different parts of the body and exercise core muscles and the pelvic area and shoulders, they work on coordinating arm and leg movements. Once your child can go forward, he can practice going left, right, backward, sideways, or over things. Move one whole side forward (arm and leg together), then the other side. Move opposite arms and legs, countering each other. Crawl over obstacles to practice coordination and balance at the same time. Let music set the rhythm and timing of your movements—a little sassy salsa or rumba, an adrenal rush from the theme of *Rocky*. When still, lift one arm straight ahead and be a "pointer." Or pull a leg straight back and up as though kicking like a mule.

When your child is comfortable with crawling, you can make up a game with these new movements. The basis of the game is to count off numbers (no higher than five) while you are crawling around and then call out a specific move or posture that you have to hold or continue for a few seconds. For instance, 1–2–3–pointer. Then your child gets to do it: 1–2–shake. Add a musical beat. The game makes you adapt your action plan to the count and the specific move.

Animals can inspire other movements, such as leapfrog or bunny hops.

If your child seems to struggle and can't feel successful, lend a hand. My colleague Ingrid Tscharnuter, a physical therapist with a center on Long Island, has developed an innovative approach to help children who have trouble with fundamental movement patterns. She calls it TAMO. (See her website at www.tamo.com.) With her approach, you stabilize one part of the child's body so that he can move other parts more naturally. A gentle hand on a key part of the leg or trunk will allow a child to move other parts that he can't quite coordinate. The touch allows the child to feel a firmer position on the floor as well as to control uncoordinated motion. Supporting a crawling child's hips or shoulders will anchor him and let him move with a more natural rhythm. Once children internalize the new rhythm, they will gradually begin to move more naturally on their own.

Finally, after mastering crawling, you graduate to standing erect and becoming bipeds—humans, lemurs, gibbons—and then walking, ultimately backward, sideways, and around in circles. Remember—simple to complex with modulating intensity and speed. Create any simple game that is fun for your child—obstacle course or treasure hunt—where you keep increasing the number of motions that the child has to do on two feet.

Walking, of course, eventually leads to running as you gradually increase the speed, and then once again you go left, right, forward, backward, over, under, and around. You can have speed modulation games: run quickly, walk slowly, walk very slowly, jog at medium speed, and then add in a change in direction. Or include other animal movements, such as kangaroo hops.

Outside, without fear of walls or furniture, use the counting game to take turns having an imaginary ball-toss (or ballet or soccer drill). To start off, you (the counter) have an imaginary ball to throw to your child. As you two run down the yard side by side but apart, you say, "1–2–hook left." You pretend to throw the ball while your child follows the directions and pretends to catch the ball. Then it's his turn. He says, "1–2–3–4–jump" and tosses the pretend ball to you, as you jump for it. Only imagination limits the combinations.

To take a break from all this activity, you can shift the focus to work on coordinating specific body parts, such as tapping both heels and then toes (or alternating them) or clapping your hands and changing the speed. Let your child set the clapping rhythm while you tap your feet, or if clapping is too difficult, your child can make a clapping noise and set the rhythm by gently slapping one hand on a thigh. He claps and you tap, then vice versa. Or you can rhythmically clap together a cappella (so to speak) or to music. He can also set the speed by perhaps playing a beat on bongo drums or tom-toms. You can then combine these exercises with voice modulation games—speaking and singing loudly, softly, super-softly. The different combinations you can create are vast.

Now that the child has gone all the way up the "evolutionary ladder," you can obviously combine running, jumping, hopping, skipping, walking, crawling, and slithering together in games. If your child aspires to some activity—dance, soccer, gymnastics, horseback riding, or bike riding—now is the time to incorporate the new strength, coordination, and planning into these aspirations. First, start the activity or sport at a very basic level so that he feels a sense of control. Then gradually move on to more complex moves so that he continues to experience the success of his new motor planning and sequencing skills.

Additional Exercises for Timing, Balance, and Coordination

Because rhythm and timing are so important to motor planning and sequencing, any form of dancing, marching, singing, or moving to music is really good. Another method is a new technology I have been involved with called the Interactive Metronome, a computer-based program for improving rhythm and timing. The child listens to rhythmic beats through earphones and performs a series of increasingly complex motor actions coordinated with the beats. He gets constant feedback about how close he is to the beat and can adjust his actions to improve his timing and coordination.

Working to improve balance and coordination gets many parts of the brain and mind working together. There's no substitute for the creativity of a child and parent for improving balance and coordination, but here are some options: running; jumping on a trampoline (jumping on two legs and then progressing to one leg); perceptual motor activities (throwing, catching, kicking); working on a low balance beam (walking and standing, standing on one leg while keeping eyes closed, throwing/catching a ball while walking on the beam); balancing on special boards and other unstable objects such as cushions; riding bikes; and jumping rope.

Balancing without using vision—blindfolded or with your eyes closed—improves cerebellum functioning, which is important for motor planning and sequencing. When you close your eyes, you depend on feedback from your proprioception, that is, the feedback you get from inside your body, in this case from the sensation of your feet against the floor. Walking, hopping, or skipping with your eyes closed—so you rely on balance, coordination, and your mental image of the room—are good exercises that you can make into fun games for children. You and your child can take turns being the guide for each other.

As we mentioned earlier, many children with motor planning and sequencing issues have trouble coordinating the left and right sides of their body. Basic activities for integrating left and right involve kicking, throwing, and catching a ball. Or you can bounce balloons on your hands (use one hand and then the other) to keep them off the ground or kick them with alternating feet. Or you can blow bubbles and try to catch them or hit them with alternating hands. Choose any activity that is fun and easy for the child to master and that alternates using both hands or feet, coordinates both sides of the body, and uses vision and motor actions together. After the child has success about two-thirds of the time, increase the speed for a more rapid, and simultaneous, practice of visual-motor and auditory-motor skills, left-right integration, and left-right balance. A very popular set of activities called "Brain Gym" (which can be found on the Internet) has many left-right games.

As you practice the three challenges—balance and coordination, rhythm and timing, and left-right integration—you strengthen the whole motor system. As long as a child has problems with those, you'll want to do a series of games a few times each day, woven in with imaginative play. This series of activities can be orchestrated by an occupational or physical therapist and then carried out by a caregiver. You can even train a teenage babysitter to implement the program with a child.

Integrating the Senses

Once your child has mastered basic motor exercises, you want to incorporate different sensory inputs. Simon Says is good practice for integrating motor actions and auditory signals: "Raise your hands, touch your knees; Simon says touch your ears, touch your shoulders; Simon says crawl through the tunnel." Such games give a kind of calisthenics for connecting all the senses in which different areas of the brain work together.

For visual-spatial and motor action (where a visual cue prompts a motion), you can use picture flash cards that show a child clapping his hands, rolling under an obstacle, and so forth. Quicken the pace. Or, from a jumble of Scrabble pieces in a box, have him choose a tile and step out the shape of the letter on the floor. Starting an "L" from the top would be three steps forward and two steps to the left. (Check back to the exercises in Chapter 9 that Isabelle did for her sight-reading.) As a child learns to read, you can use written directions—for both gross and fine motor activities.

You can even connect action and smell by offering the child whiffs of different objects—roses, vinegar, and soap—and ask him to convey what he feels is the essence of that smell by making a shape with his body. Children's creativity will surprise you!

BORED OR TOO CHALLENGED?

When a child says, "I'm bored," it doesn't always mean what we think. It can mean that the activity is too challenging. So pay attention when your child says this, but don't necessarily take it literally. Children basically like to do what's fun, which is usually what's easy for them. They don't like to do what's hard. That's OK. You adjust the activity so your child gets a sense of accomplishment—as we suggested, at least a 70 percent success rate. Then he will want to do the activity because he associates it with mastery and with feeling good about his accomplishments. If a child has less success, he will lose interest or say he is bored, which probably means that it's too difficult for him. Of course, if something is too easy and monotonous, a child could actually be bored.

Children aren't yet mature enough to reflect on a challenge and say, "I've got to tough this out in order to move ahead." When children reach the early teen years, they can take that tough attitude and work hard at dance, sports, or music training, even if their success rate is low. But at the younger ages they need a lot of encouragement.

DEVELOPING FINE MOTOR SKILLS

So far, we have focused on gross motor activities, but the same guidelines apply in improving fine motor actions, such as copying shapes, drawing, and making letters: start simply, keep the child's interests in mind, show your emotional support, and create a rhythm to the exercises. Babies begin by picking up things with the thumb and forefinger—Cheerios, for instance. Sometimes children who are good at picking things up can still take awhile to master the fine motor skills involved in crayon/pencil tasks. So the earlier you get into that, the better, but don't go beyond the child's abilities. It needs to be fun, and the child has to be able to accomplish the exercise, yes, 70 percent of the time.

The sequence for developing fine motor skills for writing and drawing begins with the child feeling comfortable holding big crayons and then making scribbles. Children often express a pleased look of, "my hands can hold something that makes something interesting." If your child has low muscle tone or a hard time grasping a writing tool, an occupational or physical therapist can teach you how to help your child with this.

Once your child enjoys scribbling, you can play copycat games by drawing basic shapes and making them into familiar objects. Start simply and make it fun, with a lot of free drawing to accompany copying shapes. Make a big circle, filling the whole page if your child prefers, and then create a face by asking him to show you where to put the eyes, mouth, and nose. But if your child seems to fumble, he can try drawing a circle with his hand on top of yours and do it with you. Or you can draw a big square box, and he can turn it into a house by making boxes for the windows and door. Take pride in whatever he produces. Children get very engaged in drawing and love an appreciative audience for their masterpieces.

When your child has a level of comfort and control, you can move on to auditory/visual/fine-motor activities, in which the child follows verbal directions and copies images. As with gross motor activities, a Simon Says drawing game is a good one: "Draw a square. Simon says draw a circle. Draw a rectangle . . . " or, "Simon says copy the picture." Another activity is for you to show your child a simple picture, take the picture away, and then see if he can reproduce it. You can choose a more complex picture for yourself and try the same thing. He gets to advise you on how you can improve.

If your child knows the alphabet, let him shape some letters from clay. Once he can do that, have him close his eyes, feel a letter, guess what it is, and then try to draw the letter. If he has a hard time guessing after feeling the shape, you can help him move his fingers over the distinct parts of the letter, and as he traces the shape, you can describe what he is feeling, in this case a "B": "Now you are feeling a straight line. Here's a round shape on the bottom and another round shape on the top that sits on the bottom one." To pull in a little gross motor connection for a young child, once he has figured out the letter and has tried to draw it, he can step it out, as he did above.

Finally, to reemphasize, throughout these activities, make sure that you have your child's interest and that the game offers plenty of opportunity to interact with you and others, as well as to bring in his own fantasy and creativity.

Can your child organize his actions?

A. How does your child move? He is . . .

1. Very floppy (low tone) and loose-jointed and doesn't try to do anything athletic
2. A little floppy but tries to run and play simple games
3. Coordinated but is not very fluid in his motions
4. A good athlete/dancer who moves with coordination and grace

continues

continued

B. Can your child follow directions when learning a new sport? He . . .

1. Gets completely confused when given directions that involve moving his body in specific ways
2. Can follow the beginning steps but can never follow the directions all the way through
3. Can follow the directions with some uncertainty and needs practice to feel comfortable with them
4. Follows directions fairly easily and learns the new motions quickly

C. How is your child's fine motor control, using handwriting as an example? My child's handwriting is . . .

1. Very messy, and he has a hard time controlling the pen or pencil
2. Somewhat messy because he has a poor grip on the implement, especially when he tries to write too quickly
3. Fairly neat, but he writes very slowly
4. Neat, and he can keep it neat even when writing a little faster

Marilyn Nolt

Organizing Thoughts

In the last chapter, you and your child worked hard, developing core strength, coordination, balance, rhythmic movement, and fine motor control—the basic tools of motor planning and sequencing. The advanced levels of planning and sequencing are physically less taxing; they provide a different kind of workout. At these levels, we focus more on the planning and sequencing of ideas that direct the movement rather than the movement itself.

Every aspect of play and learning involves planning and sequencing. In all our projects, we first have to form an action plan in our heads—a number of steps done in a certain order to achieve a desired result. With elementary school children, we can see these action plans conveyed in their pretend play—the plots behind cowboys and Indians at recess or the fresh wrinkles in a backyard adventure story that keep the action going. As children get older, planning and sequencing guide their studies—preparing for a test, juggling multiple homework assignments, or organizing and writing a long paper. But although planning problems related to movement are fairly obvious because the results can be seen, these at the higher levels of thinking are not as obvious because they are somewhat hidden. They frequently get misdiagnosed and mislabeled.

HIGHER LEVELS OF
PLANNING AND SEQUENCING

Sequencing Actions and Ideas

Children first use complex symbols (words) to express needs and thoughts in the third and fourth years. A twenty-four-month-old might scribble-scrabble with a crayon but isn't at the level of ideas yet. When a child makes kind of a circle with dots in it that looks sort of like a face and says, "That's Mommy," then she has moved into the realm of creating meaningful ideas.

Take a three-year-old girl named Jill, who is organizing the kitchen in a dollhouse, with Daddy as her helper. "Daddy, I need a stove for the kitchen." Her dad agrees that this is a very good thing to have in the kitchen.

"So is your dolly going to cook?" he asks.

"Oh, yes."

Dad then wonders, "What will the family eat on?"

"I don't know," Jill answers, "we need a table too." Looking around a bit, she finds a rectangular block to use for the table and a square block for the stove.

Dad says, "I think I hear one of your dolls make a noise. Do you think they are hungry?"

"I'll see." Off she goes to get them. And sure enough they are. "Pancakes," she says. "Their mommy will make pancakes because they like them." Daddy didn't even have to ask.

We see a series of actions—choosing furniture and organizing dinner—guided by a sequence of ideas related to the functions of the kitchen.

Being a good Floortimer, Dad continues to challenge Jill to expand the drama. Seeing Jill "feed" the doll at the table, Dad asks, "Do you think your doll is full?" Jill doesn't think so, and then Dad, in a dolly voice, says, "I'm still hungry." Jill reaches for an apple that is nearby and puts it up to the doll's mouth, two actions sequenced. Then Dolly says, "I don't like apples! I want something else!" and Jill puts down the apple, reaches for a cookie, and feeds it to the doll. Now there are three actions in a row—three actions that were supported by three ideas.

In their play, children move gradually from one step to many steps in a row. The more complex the idea, the more complex the action. The stronger the children's ability to create ideas, the more organized their actions.

Logical Thinking

At the next level of thinking, your child makes these ideas and the actions that follow more logically connected.

Jill is renovating her dollhouse. Dad is very interested and asks many questions. "Where is the dolly going to sleep?" he asks.

"She wants to sleep upstairs like me," Jill says.

Perplexed, Dad says, "But your doll house doesn't have an upstairs or any stairs." All of a sudden, Jill has a building project. They find a low stool for the "second" floor and decide that a pad of paper leaning against the stool can be the stairs. Then Jill decides to put the dolly to bed. Up she goes. Once up there, the dolly (Dad) says, "Oh, I've got to go to the bathroom! Where is it?"

"Downstairs," says Jill.

"But I need to go now," says Dad. Jill and Dad set to work fashioning an upstairs bathroom. Bit by bit, parts of the house gradually fit together logically. Spurred by Dad's curiosity, Jill takes pride in making plans and creating her dollhouse. Dad's questions expanded Jill's play, but she made all the decisions.

Putting together a farm gives Billy, a four-year-old, the same hurdles of logical connection to overcome. Making plans and carrying them out has not come easily to Billy. With his little farm having many parts and functions, he can get rather lost organizing them. Dad, not knowing about farms, asks just the right questions to help Billy figure it out. Where will the animals eat? Where do you keep the hay? How does it get up into the hay loft? Dad gently pushes Billy to connect one physical space to another, logically, with specific actions.

"What if they are thirsty," wonders Dad. Billy doesn't know.

Asking another question, Dad helps Billy answer the previous one and make the story more elaborate. "Is there a river in front of the house?" Billy pauses for a second and then says, "Yes, there is. Oh, they can drink there!"

The river poses some problems to solve, which Dad helps Billy through because thinking about alternatives is very hard for Billy.

"Well, Billy," says Dad, "what kind of river do you want it to be?"

"Oh, like the one near Grammy's house."

"Yes, I like that river too. It's really big. What if the cows want to get to the other side of the river? How can they do that?"

"I don't know," says Billy. "Maybe the cows just have to stay in the barn."

"Maybe they could do that," agrees Dad, "but what if they really need to get out? When we go visit Grammy, how do we get over the river by her house?"

"Oh," says Billy, "I know what we can do. We can build a bridge." Billy has made a plan. Dad didn't take over, but he did give Billy hints to let him figure it out himself.

We can also see logical action sequencing develop as a child's drawings become stick figures of family or friends—human figures with multiple parts, added one by one. At the same time, the child learns to make letters and numbers too, sequencing shapes together in meaningful ways. These accomplishments relate to combining ideas together logically to direct fine motor action.

When a child has difficulty executing the shapes—letters, numbers, or pictures—the key at any of these levels is to be patient. Always remember that the harder it is for a child to do something because of a weakness, the more patient you want to be, the more fun you want to make practicing, and the more initial success your child needs.

Simple conversations about everyday events also add to planning and sequencing. A little girl comes home from a trip to the park. Mom is curious about many things: does she want to go back there, why, would she like to bring a friend, who, how about tomorrow? With Mom's questions inviting her to add ideas, the little girl ends up planning her next day, partly because Mom asked and partly because her own enthusiasm about her day in the park enticed her to stay in the conversation. Her logical planning and sequencing expanded even more when packing a snack for the park. She helps Mom get the bag, find a box of juice, and make peanut butter crackers. She draws on her ideas to plan what she wants, and her eyes, ears, and hands to carry out the plans, all in logical order. Packing the lunch, she and her mother talk about shapes—a round apple, a rectangular box of juice, a triangular half of a sandwich. This little girl is more likely to remember all this than repetitive, nonexpressive activities, such as flash cards or a shape sorter, used to memorize shapes.

At kindergarten age, children can participate in more complicated games and activities. They will especially enjoy games in which they create the rules (or you create them together). When she is the creator, a child is more likely to follow a planned sequence of actions; she's more enthusiastic about it. So, before the child gets involved in team sports or formal lessons, create your own family version.

Take soccer. Unless a child is very good spatially, a big soccer field with a lot of other kids running around and kicking the ball can be disorganizing. Instead, you can start your own soccer game where the child gets four tries to kick the ball into the goal and then the parent gets four tries. Then you add rules: you two pass the ball back and forth three times before the child can kick it into the goal. Start small with a high level of success built in, make more rules together and follow them, and slowly add more rules and more participants as the child's skills improve. At the next level, your child is ready for the real rules of the game, where she learns lessons about choices.

Choice in Planning and Sequencing

As children start thinking at this level (typically between the ages of four and six), they begin realizing that there are multiple places to put that dollhouse bathroom so it is near the bedroom, and multiple places for the bridge over the river, and multiple ways to build the bridge. Many reasons, many methods. This realization is a big advance for a child because now she can consider more than one idea of how to do something and more than one idea as an explanation. Later, she'll be able to mull over different ways to prove a point in an essay. She has choices. With this understanding and improved planning and sequencing abilities, children experience a taste of freedom.

Take Harry, who is learning to play softball. He learns that if he's on base and the batter hits a pop-up ball, he probably should wait to run to the next base. Otherwise, he should take off as soon as the ball is hit. And he learns that when he's at bat, he can swing hard, bunt, or choose not to swing. Soon, when asked, he can give multiple reasons why different actions have different outcomes. A wider range of ideas comes into his head and gives him more choice, flexibility, and creativity in his actions. Advances in sequencing ideas and actions increase the complexity of Harry's logical thinking.

If a child has trouble keeping up with a game or activity as it gets more complicated, there are a couple of possible causes. The child with strong verbal sequencing skills may understand the rules but have weaker visual-spatial sequencing skills, so she gets lost and disorganized on the soccer field, for example. Or she may have the opposite problem: be able to visualize well and organize her place in the space but find it hard to remember the sequence of rules. Whichever is the problem, practice should start simply—two-step rules for verbal problems. For a child who finds it hard to figure out changing spatial settings, start with simple ball games in a defined area or set up easy obstacle courses. Then gradually make these more complex.

If an older child has trouble organizing homework, keep involving her in games or activities in which she has a lot of interest and, consequently, motivation. Use these for more basic practice in planning and sequencing. In the meantime, because homework assignments won't wait for her to improve, give her an incentive for doing them and a sanction for not doing them. But don't make it complicated, or she'll have trouble following these rules too.

Comparative and Gray-Area Thinking

Comparative and gray-area thinking open up even more planning and sequencing opportunities. A child can now line up blocks according to size (this type of comparison is called seriation) and understand number concepts (comparing what is more and less) and one-to-one correspondence (relating numbers to physical quantities). She thinks in relative terms: she can move the car a little bit, then farther, then farther still. She can set up races of different distances. She can understand time and speed, moving the car slowly, fast, then super-slowly. She can take a sequence of actions that re-quire a subtle understanding of quantity and physical space.

For practice in planning and sequencing that involves compar-isons and degrees, you and your child can plan a simple action story and draw it using stick figures. You can do one figure, and she can do the next. Or she can do the parts that are easiest for her, such as the stick body and straight arms, and you can draw in the bent running legs and the head. Here's a story. Page 1: two stick-girls are walking across a field. Page 2: the two girls in the field see a bull. Page 3: they run, and the bull runs after them. Page 4: the girls are running fast, but the bull is running faster. Will they make it? Page 5: Phew! the girls jump a fence just two steps before the bull would catch up to them. This simple story offers a feast of thinking: a plot that plans and sequences ideas, a relative sense of distance and speed, and logical drawings that connect action.

Children at the two extremes of temperaments need extra prac-tice with actions in degrees. Children who go from "zero to 60" in a moment tend to be impulsive and out of control and consequently don't sequence many actions in a row. Children who tend to repeat the same actions over and over get stuck in one pattern and don't try any new sequences.

To help children practice sequences of actions that require com-parisons or degrees, you can vary the action, speed, or direction of a game. It could be throwing a softball hard, softly, and super-softly, or throwing the ball higher or lower. Or talking through decisions about when it is better to throw the ball to first base and when to throw it to second base.

Such distinctions in the world of actions are important. From these distinctions begins to emerge an awareness of one's own body (being good at dancing and terrible at soccer) along with how easy or hard certain activities are and the different efforts required. Being able to make subtle comparisons and act accordingly lets a child better understand when a friend is wrestling with him just to fool around or in earnest because the friend is mad about losing a game. Understanding degrees of difference allows children to make judgments and organize their reactions in an effective way. Eventually these skills will help a child plan a debate or a book report, recognizing that points she can make have different levels of importance to her argument.

Reflective Thinking

At the reflective thinking level, planning one's actions or sequencing ideas is based on an internal communication with some inner standard. A child can judge her own essay or design and reflect on it as she plans the next steps. She can also reflect upon the effects her arguments or actions will have on others with whom she has a close relationship. This is an important asset because the comparative and gray-area thinking that she has learned can lead to many disagreements.

How do those disagreements get worked out? No longer is it "I'm the boss" and a push and shove, but rather with reflection and a sense of one's own values. A resolution requires understanding one's own point of view, understanding that of others, and organizing an action plan that is fair and takes account of all these factors. Take, for instance, haggling over rules. The umpire says, "Three strikes and you're out," and the batter answers, "But that wasn't a real swing!" Rules have interpretations and nuances; rarely are judgments black and white. A child realizes that she can either follow the rules; try to change the rules within the structure of the game; or point out other interpretations, which will often lead, initially, to disputes. Settling disputes requires reflecting upon alternatives and planning a resolution with an understanding of where both sides are coming from.

Self-reflection and self-evaluation work the same way, whether designing a computer game, building models, and writing essays or stories. The writer or designer plans elements ahead of time, reflects on them, carries them out, and then evaluates what she's done. In essay writing, children who have reached this stage can now diagram a logical argument (the main point and the supporting points) and then evaluate how strongly they make the case. They can put on the opponent's hat and argue against themselves in order to find and address any weak points. This strengthens logical sequencing and organization along with self-evaluation.

EXECUTIVE FUNCTIONING

Planning and sequencing are integral parts of a higher-level ability called "executive functioning." We can think of executive functioning as a composite root because it has elements of visual-spatial processing, auditory processing and language abilities, and sensory modulation, as well as motor planning and sequencing capacities. It's a cognitive skill that helps orchestrate other cognitive skills. It is crucial for solving difficult problems, for understanding subtleties of rules, for regulating and disciplining ourselves, for evaluating ourselves, for thinking abstractly, and for thinking creatively outside of the box. Here's what executive functioning does for solving a complex problem: 1) takes in information through the senses; 2) processes that information; 3) uses planning and sequencing to outline a response to the implicit challenge in the environment; and 4) executes the action in a disciplined way. Success requires a well-functioning root and trunk system.

Executive functioning is among the hardest of human endeavors, and one that many people fall short in. Why mastering this functioning is such a problem—which is on the increase—is not clear. Possible contributing factors include toxins in the environment that make it harder for the brain to sequence; the increasing complexity of our world; and lack of formative experiences that enable us to learn to sequence, plan, and take actions in an orderly and logical way.

For instance, some researchers suggest that changes in the way children play contribute as well. Free play—particularly make-believe, where children use their imaginations, make decisions, and organize their environment—lets children practice all the components of executive functioning, something that computer games, toys that create the scenarios, or extracurricular lessons do not. A big factor during make-believe is that children exercise self-regulation. They practice regulating their emotions, desires, and behaviors, something that research shows is not only hard to do but is decreasing among today's children.

Two well-known experiments point this out. The first, the marshmallow test, designed by psychologist Walter Mischel, tempted children with treats. Here are the basics: a child picked a special treat (one of which was marshmallows) and sat at a table with the treat right under her nose. An adult told the child that she had to leave the room for a few minutes, and if the child could wait to eat the treat until he returned, the child would receive two treats. Some children resisted; many others didn't. A follow-up study when the children were teenagers showed that those who resisted had higher scores on the SAT and, overall, had fewer behavior problems, both at school and at home.

In the second study conducted more than sixty years ago, children aged three, five, and seven were asked to stand perfectly still. The three-year-olds were hopeless at it, the five-year-olds managed to do it for about three minutes, and the seven-year-olds were like statues. In a recent repeat of the experiment, the three-year-olds still couldn't do it; the five-year-olds were no better than the three-year-olds; and the seven-year-olds maybe could stand still for three minutes, similar to the five-year-olds of sixty years earlier.

Many children and adults, even successful ones, have problems with executive functioning. We get overwhelmed with too many tasks; we forget to do things; we make lists, but then we forget to consult our lists; we get off-topic in conversation because we can't sequence ideas. In children, it shows up in forgetting what assignments are due and when they're due; forgetting to hand in homework; or not studying in an organized, productive way.

The principles for children developing and practicing executive functioning are similar to ones we use for planning and sequencing in general. We involve children in an activity that has a lot of interest to them, in which they are emotionally invested. It could be a play, a camping trip, a treasure hunt, or the building of a tree house. We gradually add more steps to the sequence of action or ideas. We help them incorporate as many of the senses—sight, hearing, touch, movement, and even smell—as possible. After achieving these grand plans, they are usually quite eager to report on them, step by step, explaining why they made each move or decision.

We want to give our children a strong start. For their future and for the future of the world, we want to help produce very good planners and sequencers. So the steps outlined here are important, not only to help children overcome learning and attentional problems but also to help all children develop this core ability to their maximum potential, both in the world of actions and the world of ideas.

Marilyn Nolt

12

Regulating Sensation

Sensitive or finicky. Distracted or inattentive. One kind of child may be too clued in, another kind too clued out. Children react very differently to sensations of sound, sight, touch, odor, and taste. Many need help in learning how to modulate their reactions. There are a host of reactions that can affect learning.

In the mid-twentieth century, two pioneering researchers, Sybille Escalona and Lois Murphy, described the different ways that the nervous system of babies reacts to different sensations. Then Jean Ayres, a psychologist and occupational therapist, discovered sensory differences in a group of children with learning problems. This discovery led to the term "sensory integration difficulties." Since these beginnings, occupational therapists in particular have studied and worked with children's sensory differences, creating many coping strategies.

In the preceding chapters, we discussed how to improve children's processing of sounds, their movement, and their planning and sequencing. Sensory integration approaches have a different focus: how to help children modulate sensory inputs. (The processing of touch and movement is part of the approach.) Many children have some version of a modulation problem.

Adults aren't immune either. To think about this subject a little more, ask yourselves how you rank on a sensitivity scale. For instance, maybe you dislike hubbub—chatting, music, clanging—at parties or restaurants. Your favorite sign might be EXIT. Or maybe you are part of the "turn up the volume" crowd. You can't get close enough, stay long enough, or cheer loud enough at a rock concert or football game. The more noise, the better. Maybe you don't like light touch. An uninvited tap on the shoulder feels like a major assault. Or maybe you are very physical and love to hug and wrestle. To some you seem aggressive when really you simply crave a lot of very firm touching.

With these types of sensory differences, it's easy for false impressions to flourish. If you speak to a person who doesn't respond, you may feel ignored when, in fact, the person is underreactive to sound and didn't hear you. More energy in your voice might be all that is needed. The person who did not hear you might also feel ignored. Children have the same issues but usually without the maturity or strategies to handle them. And they have to sit in a classroom for many hours a day, glued to their seats. For them, apart from a short recess, there is no socializing around the water cooler, chats on the phone, or a quick peek at a favorite Internet site so as to take a break.

In Chapter 7, where we discussed inattention, we noted that some children are overreactive, some underreactive, and some sensory-craving. This chapter expands those descriptions and gives strategies for helping these children cope with their own particular nervous system.

HOW SENSORY DIFFERENCES
AFFECT LEARNING

We'll start with children who are over- (or hyper-) reactive and who can be overwhelmed by any sensory component of the nervous system—sight, touch, hearing, smell, taste, and even how they perceive their own movement patterns (their sense of their body in space). The catalog of sensitivities can run from light touch, loud noises, or bright lights to swinging too fast on a swing set, to name a few common ones. A child can be overreactive to all these sensations or just one.

As we discuss in Chapter 17 on reading comprehension, children overloaded by the black print on a white page can have trouble reading. That may be just the beginning for these children. Classrooms bright from lights or the sun may overwhelm them, and they lose focus on class work or the directions they are given. Their attention goes out the window. The effect is similar for the child who is overreactive to sound and gets overloaded by the noise and commotion of the classroom. (Even a grating voice can be an offender.) In panic mode, a child might act silly and immature; he might shut down and retreat into a corner; he might be very cautious. But whatever the reaction, it's often a lot for the child, classmates, and teacher to handle.

The under- (or hypo-) reactive child is pretty much the opposite. Sounds may have to reach a high threshold before he reacts, whether it is someone giving him directions or chatting with him. He may not respond if you touch him lightly, only when your grasp is firmer. On a swing, contrary to the overreactive child, the underreactive child may need stronger pushing to enjoy it. These children need to be energized. They need someone to grab their attention. If the teacher doesn't realize this and doesn't pull them in, they can easily retreat into their own world.

The third category is sensory-seeking or sensory-craving and can be a feature of both types above as well as of children who have normal reactions. Some underreactive children try to counter their natural style by seeking out sensation. Some children with normal reactions seek out sensations for a boost in energy. Some overreactive children create a pattern for themselves of seeking out a lot of sensation and getting overwhelmed by it, then because they're overloaded, getting impulsive, aggressive, or silly. Mood shifts accompany this latter pattern. Children with rapidly changing moods often combine overreactivity with seeking sensations.

The sensory-seeking child has trouble sitting still in class. He needs to move and be on his feet when he's learning. He can learn to regulate himself if he has frequent breaks to get the added sensations that he needs—to run around, play games, or absorb loud, vibrant atmospheres. Recess or physical education is important for these kids as well as for those around them. If they are both overreactive and sensory-craving, they will need a lot of extra help in learning to stay calm.

Each of these patterns presents a different problem in school— for the child, classmates, the teacher, and ultimately the parents— but as a group these children are often lumped together under the label "behavior problems." By understanding these differences, we can help the children both by altering the environment and teaching the children how to control their sensitivities.

IDENTIFYING YOUR
CHILD'S SENSORY PROFILE

With the many possible combinations that can exist—under- or overreactive, a little or a lot reactive, a few triggers, a single one— what children are sensitive to isn't often obvious. You can get a picture by watching how your child reacts to different levels of stimuli for each sense. Your observations can create a sensory profile that will help design ways to enable a child to stay calm but involved. To help you do this, here is a brief systematic look at the different senses (which replaces the function of the questions at the ends of other chapters). Get out a pad of paper and sharpen your pencil.

Whether your child is a toddler or a seven-year-old, you can take a quick sensory inventory for all the senses, including the less obvious ones such as smell and taste. When a third-grader reports that the teacher's perfume is yucky, parents should take heed. Think back—did this child become irritated by Mom's perfume or Dad's strong aftershave when being cuddled? Likewise, did eating just a "few bites of (the dreaded) lima beans" at lunch upset the child for the rest of the day? Sometimes it only takes one bite.

First, consider the following list of the five senses and the related range of stimuli:

- Touch—firm pressure, light taps, scratchy clothes, hugging, and light stroking;
- Hearing—high, low, scratchy, piercing;
- Sight—bright colors, somber tones, complex patterns, straight lines;
- Taste—sour, sweet, tangy, bland;
- Smell—strong food odors, perfumes, chemicals in the air.

An associated kind of sense affects what is called the proprioceptive system, affected by any movement—swinging, being tossed in the air, or carnival rides.

Pain, whether a little scratch or a big cut, can also upset and overwhelm a child. Children differ in their reactions to pain.

How does your child react to each stimulus for that sense? Think through the list below and reflect. Here are five reactions. This range of reactions and their interpretations below are fairly uniform for all the senses. Your child:

- really craves any of these sensations;
- really hates any of them;
- is bothered but can hold it together for a short time;
- doesn't mind unless it continues for a long time;
- doesn't really even notice one way or the other.

For instance, if a child loves loud sounds, he may crave that sensation, which suggests that he has a sensory-craving side—maybe not with everything, but with certain sounds. Spoken to in a monotone or a soft voice, he's bored and inattentive. And in a quiet environment, he may try to create the sounds he thrives on, which is not a good situation in school, camp, church, or any number of other places one can think of. The child who hates noise will be overwhelmed by a boisterous school event, a noisy classroom, even recess. If the classroom is a little chaotic, this child loses attention and, if overwhelmed, may act up in some way that the teacher will probably find objectionable.

The child who doesn't like noise but can cope for awhile then ultimately gets irritated is on middle ground. He has more resources and more time to figure out how to control an uncomfortable atmosphere. It doesn't just hit him. He has an opportunity to figure out where his limits are and how to keep within them so that he doesn't get upset by the overstimulation. But this will require practice because the ability to cope can easily get swept away from a child.

The child who doesn't notice may be the most unflappable kid around. Or he may be isolated and need to be pulled in.

IMPORTANT: A child with auditory processing problems could also have auditory sensitivities (or visual processing problems and visual sensitivities, etc.). If so, you have to make sure that you use sounds that are easy for him to work with. The same goes for motor planning and sequencing. If your child has motor planning problems and is sensory-craving, be ever vigilant that the planning and sequencing exercises give him plenty of opportunity to move about but not lose control.

COUNTERBALANCING

One general approach to helping children who need to learn to regulate their reactions to senses is counterbalancing. We discussed this in Chapter 4, when in no uncertain terms Rachel refused to eat her mashed potatoes. Her dad had a few choices to try to change her mind: one was to get mad at her and tell her she had to eat them; another was to calm her down and playfully induce her to try some. Her wise dad chose the latter, that is, he counterbalanced her angry mood with his playful one, got her attention, and enticed her to try some. With his actions, he balanced out her mood of the moment. For the children described in this chapter, the way to reengage them is by counterbalancing the individual child's reaction—energize the zoned-out kid; soothe the revved-up one—and then relate in a way that promotes equilibrium.

Do you remember Jeremy? He built a wonderful fort and laser shield a few chapters back. By that time he was fairly organized, but when younger, he overreacted to certain sounds and also craved other kinds of sensation. He needed a lot of touch and movement and could get impulsive. He was a difficult mix, driving his parents crazy. He and I made a game of marching, skipping, and running to soft music, on the beat, on every other beat, then a half-beat quick step. Together, we made up rules. Sometimes we swung our arms, then we had to hold them up without moving them, sometimes we put our hands on our hips, and sometimes we hopped with our hands on our knees. Jeremy learned ways to modulate his movements and to regulate the reactions that got out of control with certain sounds and when he craved sensation.

SENSORY PROBLEMS AND THE STAGES OF THINKING

Attention and Engagement

A child who overreacts or underreacts to something can get blocked from being calm or forming relationships right from the beginning. These first two crucial thinking levels, attention and engagement, are exactly where the trouble shows up first.

In an underreactive child—completely laid back—a mother may remember having to use her energy to pull him in so that he paid attention. Otherwise he got lost in his private world. With such help, an underreactive child discovers how wonderful the people in his world are so that he wants more. (With this kind of child, we need to make sure that our enthusiasm isn't counterproductive, that it doesn't unintentionally overwhelm him.) For the overreactive child—the squirmy, energized kid—Mom can soothe and calm with gentle tones and movement until he can pay attention. She can engage him softly. These children then also learn how nice it is to take in the world and to have a gentle rhythm with a loved one that deepens the relationship.

Sometimes children outgrow these sensitivities. But when they persist, the fussy or finicky baby becomes a fussy or finicky toddler, and then a fussy or finicky preschooler, and so on.

Attention and engagement happen naturally for many children. Whatever learning problems there are often occur a little further downstream. But with an over- or undersensitive child, big or little, these first two levels of attention and engagement will remain the important ones. As you play, talk, or interact with your child, no matter how old, always remember to check whether he is calmly engaged and in control of his emotions and behavior.

Communicating Effectively

A calm and attentive child can respond to gestures and expressions and initiate new ones to create a circular flow. But an over- or underreactive child easily gets out of sync and loses the exchange of gestures, sounds, or facial expressions. Such a child needs a wooer who not only keeps the flow going but, again, who counterbalances. When an overreactive child gets carried away, Dad can counterbalance by softening his voice. When the underreactive child drifts off into his own world, Dad can counterbalance by increasing his energy and making his gestures more dynamic (just not too much). With sensitive children, such counterbalancing empowers the child. A child feels Dad's effect on him. He realizes that he can interact with Dad to re-create a sense of balance rather than be the victim of his sensory system. When he gets "out of step," his parents' response teaches him that he has an impact on the world and can master it.

Problem Solving

At the level of shared social problem-solving, a child uses his signaling system in more complex ways. He organizes patterns; he communicates even more purposefully. He knows what he wants and can get you to help. At this stage, the underreactive, overreactive, or sensory-seeking child needs support in asking for help and expanding his sensory world in an organized way. Otherwise, he may do what comes naturally, which is giving into his reactions.

The cautious, overreactive child who only wants to do quiet activities can gradually move to more assertive ones that use his muscles and engage his senses. Initially, this can be as simple as encouraging a trip to the library and back. Once there, or at places such as a science museum or park, a passive couch potato may morph into an active explorer.

For the child running around aimlessly seeking sensation, you can make up a movement game with modulated fast and slow components—similar to the Evolution Game described earlier—where he has to move in certain ways to achieve certain purposes. You and he can pretend you are walking through really thick, gooey mud, slowly pulling your back leg forward and taking a big step, and slowly pulling the opposite leg up. Then you hit a patch of ice, fast and slippery, where your feet slide around and your body tries to keep balanced. The child will get more invested if he gets to create his own game that his mom or dad has to follow. Later on this child will be able to say "Hey, let's go out and kick the soccer ball" or "Let's go dancing," rather than just act out or be impulsive without any warning. On his own, he will be able to organize his need for activity.

To help a child with sensory problems act in purposeful ways to get what he needs and wants, parents need to help him stay calm and regulated or stimulated as the case may be. His successes will further motivate him. He needs both the freedom and the control to take advantage of his natural interests.

Expressing Sensory Needs with Words and Ideas

The more articulate the child, the more he can control his own sensory environment: "Mommy, that's too loud," or "Daddy, let's wrestle!" Through pretend play, he can explore sensory likes and dislikes or feelings that are overexcited or uninvolved. His dolls or animals can be scared of bright lights or want to run wild. The child can put words and ideas to his sensory feelings so that he now symbolizes—using words and gestures—what his inner world is like. He can announce his needs: "I want to run!" or "I feel antsy right now," or "There's too much going on." With this information, a caregiver can counterbalance more effectively, while the child, getting help, experiences his own impact on the world—developing a greater sense of mastery.

Logical Thinking

When children talk about the feelings that overwhelming sensations stir up, these feelings become less scary and intense. They can compare their fantasies with reality. As children become more aware of their inner world, feelings won't become frightening nightmares. In other words, if the child can talk about being afraid that the loud noise will crush him or that he'll burst apart if he doesn't move, he's less likely to be scared by it.

Creating play scenarios in which overreactive children can pretend to be a monster or a villain can help them gradually to become comfortable being assertive. In the safety of pretend play, along with a parent's guiding hand, the child can expand his sensory world—an overreactive child practicing to be more assertive and a sensory-craving child practicing to be more aware and empathetic. This way the child gets tools he can use for the hard work of counterregulating his reactions. Then he can use these behaviors in the real world.

Sensory Problems at Higher Levels of Thinking

The process of sensory modulation becomes even more subtle and nuanced as we move up the ladder to multicausal, gray-area, and comparative thinking. At these levels, a child can describe which sounds are scary, how scary they are, and how one scary sound compares to another. He can fine-tune his control of his sensory world by thinking through why he likes riding horses better than playing field hockey or reading. And, finally, when he gets to reflective thinking, he can even tell you that today, due to not sleeping well the night before, he's more sensitive than usual: "I'm more nervous today," or "It's harder for me to pay attention today." And then he can take conscious corrective action on his own—"I'd better get more sleep tonight," or "I need to listen to music to calm down."

MASTERING SENSORY PROBLEMS

The goal is for children to become the master of their sensory difference rather than the victim. You know as an adult that knowledge of your preferences is powerful—the security of knowing the kinds of touch you enjoy, the kinds of music, parties, or activities. This gives you control over your reactions. For a child, too, that is reassuring. A cautious child may actually find that he enjoys contact with other kids as long as he's not being surprised and can be in charge of it.

Occupational therapists have worked out a number of techniques to help children regulate their sensory systems more effectively (for example, applying firm pressure for an overreactive child who's sensitive to light touch; soothing sounds for the child who's overreactive to sound; more subdued lighting for one who's overreactive to light; and rhythmic movement with firm pressure for the child who's very reactive). Diane Lewis, a gifted speech pathologist and therapist who coauthored the *Affect-Based Language Curriculum* with me, found that using spandex swings, which provide tactile and proprioceptive support, can facilitate language development in some overreactive children. This kind of movement helps keep them regulated.

Children who are underreactive need a lot of sensory stimulation, such as massage and being spoken to in an energetic voice. Also, movement helps to organize their systems and make them more aware of their surroundings.

The sensation-craving child needs limits coupled with times for organized action. He needs to respect others by keeping chaos to a minimum. At the same time, he needs to find ways to get a lot of touch, sound, and movement throughout the day. You can let him know that you recognize his desire to fidget or make noise but teach him that there are special times to move around and special times to be quiet.

As children become more verbal, it's important to help them understand and describe what their sensory systems feel like. How do loud noises make you feel? Are they exciting, or do they make you feel overloaded or overwhelmed? What does it feel like when you want to move and yet everyone's being quiet and you have to be still? What does it feel like when you're finally given the chance to move around during recess or during your breaks? Verbalizing their feelings and sensations helps children to master their sensory systems.

Should your child require additional help, find an occupational therapist who works with the sensory system. Those who receive special training in this area refer to themselves as "sensory-integration trained."

In summary, we begin by recognizing how a particular child's sensory system reacts. Then, we help the child regulate himself through attention and engagement while we stay ready to counterregulate. Next, we let the child feel the impact he can have on the world, and we help him expand his sensory world. The child's mastery of his senses increases when he can use ideas and words to express his feelings. Then we fine-tune his mastery through comparative thinking, gray-area thinking, and finally reflective thinking applied to how he views his reactions. At each stage, as we strengthen the child's thinking in regard to his sensations—and the feelings that go along with these sensations—the child understands himself better and improves the mastery of his sensory system.

13

Making Sense of What We See

In this chapter on visual-spatial processing and visual-spatial thinking, we draw heavily on the work of Harry Wachs, who worked with Jean Piaget in the mid-twentieth century. Wachs and his colleague Hans Furth were pioneers in extending Piaget's theories to visual-spatial thinking in their book, *Thinking Goes to School.*

To make sense of what we see and to use what we see to think, learn, and solve problems, we must process this visual information. We use vision to be aware of how our own body works, to understand how our body relates to others and to our physical environment, and to make sense of this environment. For example, we walk into a library filled with rows of bookshelves. Some aisles are empty, some filled with people—a fairly common scene. We see the shape of the room, our position in it, the objects that are near and far, and any signs identifying the rows. We take it all in and almost instantaneously determine the path to reach our desired spot, deciding whether to thread through busy aisles or to go the long way around and avoid the crowd. For most of us, processing all this information is automatic.

If we go up a few notches on the visual-spatial difficulty curve, say, catching a ball in the outfield, the processing is continuous and more complicated. We have to make split-second judgments using both visual information and experience. To run to the correct place on the field and get into a position to make the catch, we map the dimensions of the field in our mind, we track the ball with our eyes, and we plan and coordinate the movements of our arms, hands, torso, feet, and head to be ready to catch that ball. With some practice, many of us can perform this task pretty well.

For some children, however, processing all this information is not so automatic or so fast. In the library, they can't size up the space or make a map of where they need to go. They don't know how to turn or twist their bodies to make it through tight spots. On the field, they don't make it to quite the right spot in enough time (assuming there is time), and they don't have their hands in the right place. They become confused and disorganized. They can't organize the space in their minds or organize the movement of their bodies in the space. A child playing soccer who can't keep a mental map of the field and the constantly changing positions of the players and the ball won't end up in a position to kick the ball or block the shot.

Visual-spatial skills involve not only sight but also motor planning, sequencing, sound, and touch. A blind person can make a mental map of a room by sound and touch. In this chapter, we show how the dimensions fit together to help the child define a space and figure out how to move about in it. Do you remember Andy from the introductory chapter on the roots? He went upstairs to find his shoes but, not having a good physical sense of his room, gave up and got waylaid by his favorite toy after checking one spot. He didn't find the shoes because he really didn't understand the spatial features of the room. That there was a space under the bed that he could reach into if he lay down and stretched his arm out never occurred to him.

A child to whom visual-spatial processing does not come easily may need help with:

- mapping a space with all that it contains, including the location of objects within that space;
- planning and sequencing movement needed to navigate the space and reach a goal;
- feeling where her body and limbs should be in space to execute a movement, such as when the body spins around the center axis or the right arm crosses the left side to reach for an object;
- tracking moving objects.

Whether when playing with soccer balls, Frisbees, or the much-loved cat, any exercises to encourage all this should involve you or members of the family along with favorite toys and activities. Only then will they have emotional meaning to her and stick with her.

STAGES OF VISUAL-SPATIAL PROCESSING

Attending to Sights

Noticing the world is our first step. Newborns are drawn to faces. When they hear a mother's or father's voice, they turn to find their faces. Very quickly, they see that the series of shapes that they will later learn to call a nose, mouth, ears, and eyes equals a pattern, a face. Because newborn babies can discriminate very basic patterns, the human brain seems to be prewired for that ability. From this early beginning, babies develop the ability to make sense of their world.

The importance of observing is critical at all ages. Curious children take in everything they see, absorbing details, patterns, and motion. On a nature walk, it may be the color and shape of flowers, the texture of the bark on the trees, the shape of the leaves, or the little maple seeds with wings. Animals always attract a child's attention: squirrels chasing each other, a puppy chewing a toy, a police officer's horse. On a long car trip, watching and counting is a perfect opportunity to entertain bored children. How many things that are red can they find in ten minutes? How many animals? How many trucks? Whatever we're doing with our children—going on the subway, visiting a museum, or just shopping for groceries—we can ask them to tell us what they find interesting.

But if children get overloaded by visual stimuli (those we discussed in the previous chapter), they need to be exposed to new sights in a modulated way. They can then stay calm and not exceed their tolerance. If bright lights or colors overwhelm a child, a carnival may not be the best outing, or at least not for any length of time. But for children at the opposite end who are underreactive, the to-do of a carnival may be perfect.

But even an overreactive child can enjoy coordinating sight with the other senses. A beautiful garden, with all its colors and shapes, smells, textures, the buzz of bees and flutter of butterflies, might be a good place to start. Or your child might prefer the petting zoo.

Engaging the Visual World

All the games of early childhood offer visual excitement and encourage visual skills. Games from Peek-a-Boo to treasure hunts require observation and a sense of space. Take a child angling for a ride on Daddy's back. Dad, moving about the room, is defining the space for his daughter. She is watching him, tracking his movements, planning and sequencing her own, and getting a sense of how he moves in space as she tries to catch him.

Interaction and Communication

Games, such as kicking a ball back and forth or playing tag, add increased awareness of the visual-spatial world—where things are relative to where the child is. The flow between parent and child, or sibling and child, as their arms, heads, and body move in synchrony lets the child sense a relationship with objects in space. There is fluidity, balance, physical coordination, and motor planning all because the child sees something that intrigues her. She uses these qualities to communicate across space and to navigate the space.

Even for a preverbal child, you can describe the position of a toy that you are holding up for her to grab. "It's up; it's down. It's high; it's low. It's over here; it's over there. It's behind me; it's in front of me." You show and describe; she reaches and takes. Long before the child understands words, she experiences, through vision and sound, different positions of the toy, the beginning of the "Where is it?" game.

In the visual-spatial world, two-way communication helps the child become aware of her body in space and in relationship to other people and objects, which may also be moving. She tracks, plans, moves, and judges the distance to other players. Before knowing the concept of seconds and minutes, she also gets a sense of time—that it takes time to get there. In this way, the concepts of space and time form experientially for the child.

If a child has mild problems with motor planning (that is, she can move her whole body, even if awkwardly), she can get this kind of practice with exercises such as the Evolution Game described earlier. To make it more fun, add an enticement—a toy or treat. If a child has more severe motor problems, the physical tasks should be as simple as necessary, such as just turning and looking or using tongue movements. If the movement builds on a communication with others and movement in space, the child can develop a visual awareness of the environment.

Visual Problem-Solving

As soon as children can look for things, try to get things, and ask for your help with gestures and words, they will be learning where things are in space. If her special stuffed animal is missing, the child has a strong incentive to search her room to find it. The special toy invests the space with meaning. At the problem-solving level, children are ready to put the spatial terms they have heard into operation. These characterize the space. The position of desirable objects does as well.

Treasure hunts, as we said, are made for visual-spatial problem-solving. There are two kinds, the intentional ones and the unintentional ones. Children probably have the most experience with the latter—something special is often missing. But experience with the former can help children deal more successfully with the latter. With a small child, you can hide an object of great interest while your child is watching. You obviously hide the glittery plastic star in your pocket or underneath you: "I'm putting the star under me. Can you find it?" When that becomes easy, it's on to less obvious hiding places accompanied by verbal cues: "Is it under me, behind me, under my foot?" She gets to push you about while you make suggestions of where it might be. Is it in your hand? In your pocket? Are you sitting on it so that she has to nudge you a little? An added complication is to hide the star on yourself and crawl so that she has to chase after you to find the star. Interesting hiding places increase the attention to detail.

Make the game multisensory. If the child has a hard time orienting to the space, you can add a sound cue—"Beep-beep. I'm over here." Or give the "hot" or "cold" clue. Alternatively, choose a "treasure" that has an interesting texture or smell or requires a different movement, such as reaching or stretching, to find it. As the child gets older, encourage actions that use the left and right hands together and the left and right feet together—crawling, climbing, running, or jumping. As the hunt expands into a larger physical space, so does the child's internal image for that space—how things connect, which movements help to navigate the objects within the room, and how the room functions overall.

For children with visual impairments, we help them to construct a visual-spatial world from sound, touch, and their own movement. A verbal child could describe what something would look like by touch, smell, size, and taste (if appropriate). She can figure out a room's dimensions by walking around the walls and can locate an object in the space by the sound it makes when tapped (knocking on a wooden table, for instance). The sound will shift as she changes her position in the room, getting louder as she walks over to touch it. She forms her own visual-spatial map of an area and, with verbal cues and sounds, can go on a treasure hunt.

A key piece of visual problem-solving is the recognition of patterns. This includes imitation of behavior as well as language. Mommy comes home, puts her briefcase down, and then takes off her shoes and rubs her feet. Pretty soon little Susie takes off her own shoes and rubs her feet. Imitation is one way we learn complex social and intellectual skills. Susie's imitation of her mother involves close observation and a multistep action plan, fairly complicated visual-spatial problem-solving.

Pattern recognition lets children figure out how pop-up toys or other mechanical objects work. This thinking ability helps them to master their world, such as figuring out how to take a stool over to the bookshelf to reach a toy. These problem-solving actions require not only motor planning and sequencing but also understanding how the world works in terms of where things are and how to find them—mapping the visual-spatial world.

"Functional understanding" of the world is another form of pattern recognition. Through observation and imitation, children begin to understand the function of physical objects through patterns of use. The pattern is eventually labeled a "doll" or a "telephone," but the child sees the pattern and understands the function of the object long before she can label it. Even a sixteen-month-old child will imitate adults on the phone, putting it to her ear and making noises; she understands that its function is to communicate.

Perhaps the child has her own comb, brush, and mirror in a little bag. She stands next to Daddy while Daddy combs his hair. The child finds her own comb among her things so she can imitate Daddy. She begins to relate objects to their function as well as their color, shape, texture, or just general fascination. Kids naturally gravitate toward imitation, especially when it gets them what they want.

Visual Symbols and Ideas

A child at this level has already begun to develop a sense of space and how to move in it. She has seen how objects have patterns and functions. She can differentiate one object from the other. Now she makes the experience more conceptual by labeling objects. You have been doing this for her all the time. All the familiar activities in the playground and the sights on a walk have labels—the plants and the animals and the ground and the sky—and as the child has grown up hearing you describe them and asking questions herself, the labels have become familiar.

Language lets a child use symbols to organize the physical world. Gradually over a couple of years, she learns how to symbolize the spatial dimensions she sensed earlier and then practiced with "Where is it?"—under the couch, on your head, in the closet. With these visual-spatial words, she solves problems more easily. Hearing and using labels, the child can increasingly form ideas of what "in," "above," "beyond," or "below" look like.

Incorporating construction sets in pretend play is a boost to spatial ideas. Building blocks create different objects in space—something simple such as a fence for the horses or a house for the family. The scope for visual imagination is endless. As the child builds, she and you can label objects in terms of their relationships: distance, quantity, height, and so on.

As children slowly get the sense of quantity and the dimensions of space, they begin to develop higher cognitive capacities. One is what we call "one-to-one correspondence," that "three" (a symbol) equals those three blocks in the pile. This ability generally comes in later in other senses, but in the visual-spatial world, it's easier. Three blocks versus two blocks, very concrete objects, are easier to recognize than saying three words versus saying two, a more conceptual count. Children also begin to understand that the shapes they see (the lines, circles, and half-circles) make letters, which correspond to sounds that blend together to make words. In this way, strong visual-spatial abilities make a foundation for more formal academic activities.

Logical Sorting

Your child's budding use of symbols gets more of a workout as she connects ideas together logically to make sense of the world and begins to answer "why" questions. Being able to sort and classify, which builds on recognizing patterns, is part of this new understanding. If you don't see this skill developing in your child, a little extra fun practice can help her progress to this new level.

Multicolored blocks of different shapes are useful here. A child can search for one of each color and one of each shape. Or two children can take a specific number of turns and see who gets the most different blocks. The challenge can be to build houses with blocks of different shapes. If you ask your child about her favorite shape and why, she can now give you a reason, but usually only one at this point. It is the same with her favorite color and her favorite house design. Just through sorting and building, children begin to see how the spatial world is configured and how many choices there are. These kinds of games are great for establishing higher-level symbolic pattern recognition.

At this age, children also expand on the idea of one-to-one correspondence (i.e., counting), especially when they are invested in the object. So if there are three Oreo cookies stacked like a tower or three lying side by side like a train, you can ask the child which group she wants. If she prefers the cookie tower, leave three cookies in this one and add a fourth to the other (or vice versa). She may not know that four is bigger than three conceptually, but she'll probably figure out pretty quickly that she now likes the group with the most cookies. She begins to realize that it's not how the cookies are arranged but how many there are that actually matters. As children become more verbal at this stage of connecting ideas together, they can begin to learn to count: there are 1, 2, 3 cookies stacked up, but 1, 2, 3, 4 cookies lined up side by side.

Once children see bigger patterns and can label them, sorting works with everything. In the grocery store, a child can understand, "Let's put the tall things (bottles) in one corner of the cart, round things (fruit) in another, small boxes in the middle, and big boxes underneath." Maybe even sorting toys and putting them away can be made into a fun game.

Remember in Chapter 11, on organizing thoughts, how Jill needed to build stairs in her doll house and Billy had to figure out where to put a bridge over the river at his farm? These children were logically connecting visual-spatial ideas, planning and sequencing the functional parts. Building a block or Lego house is great practice in seeing how all the parts connect together and make sense, as is a treasure hunt where there are increasingly complicated verbal clues to visual-spatial differences. If the spatial components connect one to the other logically, the child will see the relationships of objects in space.

When we gave examples of games for planning and sequencing thoughts in Chapter 11, we used the example of children inventing their own rules because rules need to have a logical sequence. Because athletic games involve a playing area, a visual-spatial field, the same principles apply here, whether the rules are invented for soccer or for batting balloons back and forth. These games can be as simple or elaborate as the child wants. If the child has trouble orienting herself on the field, start small and with simple movement patterns. In a delineated space, with a visual boundary line, she stands close and parallel to the line and kicks a ball a short distance to a partner. Gradually she moves inward toward the middle of the field away from the marked boundary. She and her partner can also kick at an angle to the line so that she has a reference point and gets a sense of distance from different perspectives. Your supporting the child with a description of her actions helps her to combine visual-spatial sequencing with verbal sequencing, which makes the spatial learning more conceptual.

With any game where the child sets the rules, you can, in good Floortime style, ask questions that gradually increase the complexity. For instance, "Can you throw the ball against the far wall and catch it again? Can you catch it after a second bounce?" Spatial directions little by little encourage balance and coordination, left/right integration, and complex sequencing with many steps in a row. As the child creates new rules and movements, she uses all her sensory channels together by describing the logic of the game, finding her place in the space, using her motor system, and planning and sequencing—all from connecting visual-spatial ideas together. In the games that she plans, make sure that she doesn't make them too complex. She is more likely to stay engaged if she succeeds 70–80 percent of the time.

Multicausal Visual Thinking

Without your even noticing, children will soon be designing more intricate houses (connecting more rooms), creating more sophisticated rules for games (leading friends through complex treasure hunts that require subtle visual cues), and recognizing larger patterns (quickly seeing and appreciating the positions on a basketball court).

They can now identify the different qualities of objects. If they look at a group of objects and then try to identify them blind-folded, using touch or smell (or taste if it's food), they can figure out which object it is. They are learning to construct a visual image from the other senses, which actually strengthens visual-spatial problem-solving.

Children at this level might find it a fun challenge to see how many logical designs of cars, houses, or planes they can make from a set number of different-shaped blocks. Or they can create interesting-looking abstract designs. Such designs get children into multicausal thinking in spatial dimensions—developing many causal relation-ships between the same shapes.

As we described earlier, the Lindamood-Bell approach to help-ing children with reading skills is to have children make the shape of letters with their bodies or walk out the shape on the floor. Chil-dren can symbolize words, such as the word "dog," by walking or dancing or crawling the letters out, by writing the letters in the air with their hands, and by creating letters with blocks or Legos. Us-ing these multiple ways of symbolizing letters or ideas makes them more meaningful and helps children connect more of their sensory and motor worlds to what they see.

Comparative and Gray-Area Visual Concepts

Whether playing with cookies or clay, children will eventually see that they can take a piece of clay, for instance, and make it into a round ball or stretch it out into a snake and it's the same amount of clay. They soon learn that the amount of liquid in a tall, thin glass and the amount of liquid in a fat, short glass can be the same. Gray-area thinking can operate in the visual sphere, looking at objects in relative proportions and in multiple dimensions.

Children learn these concepts the best—and have the most fun—by experimenting with the physical world so they see firsthand how space, weight, quantity, and shape can all be transformed. Set up your home "science lab" with clay, Play-Doh, water, glasses of various sizes, scales, and weights. Let your child be free to experiment. Soon you will be called in to watch the amazing feats and discoveries she has made.

For a child who isn't drawn to such activities or who has trouble with understanding visual relationships or math, you can offer some games. Start off with two squares of clay that are exactly the same; have her roll one piece into a ball and the other piece into a long object, such as a snake or log. Then ask her, "Which has more clay, the snake or the ball?" Juice is another convenient example. Start off with two similar glasses with the same amount of liquid. Pour one into a long, thin glass and the other into a short, fat glass and ask her which glass has more juice. If she can't tell, pour them back into the similar glasses and try again. It may not come immediately. Ask questions: "So, what do you make of the fact that you started off with the two things that were the same and now you're telling me there's more of one than the other? Are you a magician? How did you do that?"

A complicated twist on this is to have the child create different shapes out of clay—a snake, a ball, a square, a tower. Then ask which one has more clay in it. The child can do that by experimenting—by molding each clay creature back into a ball and then arranging them from the smallest to the largest. This game illustrates visual relationships, or what Piaget called "seriation tasks." This is a basic foundation for mathematical reasoning.

Through their own experimenting and these kinds of games, children begin to realize that looks can be deceiving and that they have to take a multidimensional approach to figure out whether one quantity of something is more or less than another. This understanding matures over a long time.

With real objects, children at this level of comparative and gray-area visual-spatial thinking can develop a sense of simple multiplication. They already have a sense of quantity (numbers as symbolic meaning) and how taking away one unit or adding one changes how much of something that they get. If your child has a friend over and each wants to have an apple, she will probably be able to tell you how many apples that is. If there are three children and each gets two pieces of cheese, you can give her six pieces and, by counting out "one for you" and "one for you," she sees that they each get two. What happens if one child doesn't want any? How much do the other two get? Making it simple and using real objects in real-life situations give the arithmetic process physical meaning. You can then show your child how to represent it with numbers, even labeling the processes of adding and subtracting and multiplying.

Strengthening visual-spatial capacities simultaneously strengthens the sense of quantity and sense of time because these depend on being able to see and understand how space is organized. Learning the terms for big and little, more and less experientially, not just as memorized definitions, makes them part of a child's sense of the world. The same process occurs with understanding the concept of time. Time exists in a feeling sense, and we relate it to experiences we have in the real world, like an hour-long TV show or an hour for lunch. That's how we develop our internal sense of time. So when you say, "Three seconds to launch the rocket," that teaches a sense of time within the context of play.

Design expands at this level too. Harry Wachs has developed a number of games where children copy designs from different perspectives—not as the designs look to the child but how they look in mirror image or upside down from the perspective of the person sitting across the table. The child has to transform what she sees and draw the design as the other person sees it, rather than just to copy it. The harder the design, the harder the transformation. Here's the picture of the front of a house. What does the back of the house look like? Can she draw it? Space is visual, but it can be represented in many forms. A child can talk about how she wants to organize her room; she can draw a picture of it; she can include her brother and herself playing in the room; she can act out how she will move about the room. As children's thinking becomes increasingly complex in terms of making connections between ideas, we want to encourage them to use multiple forms of expressing those ideas.

Reflective Thinking

With reflective reasoning, children can look at construction, designs, and drawings and judge their quality. They can not only design a fort or tree house but also evaluate how the style compares with their friends' or their own house and reflect on how these might work. They use their imagination to draw fantastic, futuristic airplanes and rocket ships. They can read about great coaches and put their own twist on the "pick and roll" or some other maneuver. As they grow into their teen years, they get better and better at these abilities. We want to encourage kids to be artists, designers, and architects and to experiment—while making sure that their ideas are logical and that they evaluate and improve their own work.

The visual-spatial world is complex and can have many different dimensions. The key concepts in developing higher-level visual-spatial processing skills are, first, helping children to invest themselves in all parts of their visual-spatial world by encouraging them to explore space for emotionally meaningful reasons (i.e., finding something they want). The next steps are learning about all the different spatial dimensions, being creative in using space, and creating logical connections between different spatial entities. Then we want to help children move up the ladder to multicausal, gray-area, and reflective thinking with space—such as (literally) seeing things from other people's perspectives—and then to learn the relationships of objects in space. All this will develop the foundations for math, science, and the visual and movement arts. The ability to comprehend the world lies not just in verbal understanding but also in visual and spatial understanding.

How well does your child navigate different kinds of spaces?

A. **If you misplace your car keys, would you readily expect your child to be able to find them? My child . . .**

1. Would probably not be able to find them and probably wouldn't try. She is always losing her own things and is not able to find them
2. Would probably try but doesn't have a good sense of where misplaced things might be, so she looks in all the obvious places
3. Has some feel for the various possibilities where things could be
4. Has a good sense of all the nooks and crannies and is thorough in examining them systematically

B. **Is your child clever at putting things together or constructing things, from forts made out of couch cushions to rudimentary tree houses? My child . . .**

1. Tends to watch as others put things together because she just doesn't know how to begin
2. Tries, but the results are not satisfactory to her
3. Has an idea of how it all fits together but can't always make it work
4. Really likes to construct things and does a good job

continues

continued

C. You show your child that you have put the same amount of her favorite beverage in a tall, skinny glass and in a short, wide glass. You ask your child which she wants to drink and why. (The conservation principles of volume, length, and number come in around age seven.) My child would . . .

1. Choose the tall, thin glass and say it has more
2. Choose the short, wide glass and say it has more
3. Not be able to decide
4. Say it doesn't matter. They are both the same.

Marilyn Nolt

Integrating All the Roots
The Sidwell Friends Nutrition Project

By Richard Lodish, Ed.D., with
Monica Sorensen and Liz Wilson

Monica Sorensen and Liz Wilson, Sidwell Friends kindergarten teachers, developed a delightful and imaginative social studies unit on food. The goals of the unit were 1) to encourage children to form an open-minded attitude about trying new foods; 2) to encourage healthy food choices in everyday life; and 3) to influence the types of foods that class parents brought to school for special events. The unit incorporated language arts, visual arts, math, and science. But most important, as one teacher said, "Our curriculum resonated with the children because they became emotionally invested in what we were studying."

THE FOOD PYRAMID

The project started out during story time with a sampling of books about food, which were also on display for individual reading so that the children gained a general background. They could page through *The Seven Silly Eaters*, *I Will Never Eat a Tomato*, *Good Enough to Eat: A Kid's guide to Food and Nutrition*, and many others. The project quickly became hands-on with an assignment for the children to record what they ate for dinner and then to draw a picture of each item in a box on a piece of paper and to label it. In school the next day, the children cut out each of the boxes, spread them all out on a table, and sorted them into six categories, which they collectively decided on. Grasping the idea of grouping similar items, they came up with noodles, fruit, vegetables, food from other countries, and other (miscellaneous).

The teachers then introduced the idea of the food pyramid and had the children compare their groups to those in the food pyramid, which weren't so different. With the idea of the food pyramid made clear, each child was assigned to one of its food groups. Each team then selected the homework food pictures that fit into their food group and glued them onto a large piece of paper. The impressive result was a huge food pyramid.

The children proudly hung their masterpiece on the classroom wall and in so doing, quickly created one of the main foci of the classroom. As visitors, big and small, came to the room, all received nutritional instruction from eager kindergartners. To explain the food pyramid became a cherished activity.

The nutrition project involved many art projects. The children drew a wall mural of children eating, they learned and illustrated a poem about the food pyramid, and they drew a still-life from a basket of real food. This last one had a grand payback. When the drawings were done, the teachers cut up the actual food in the basket and set it out on platters. One afternoon the children sampled walnuts, bananas, grapes, broccoli, Swiss cheese, a baguette, and dark chocolate—a representative from each of the food groups. (At this time, the food pyramid included a category "fats, oils, and sweets," hence the dark chocolate.)

In the past, many of the children would have turned their noses up at some of these tidbits. But few did this time. These were now the foods they knew about and related to. Their curiosity was sharpened. They took a bite.

Now that they knew about the food pyramid and had expanded their own food choices, the class engaged in an experiment to discover how well they balanced their meals. For three days, each one of them recorded what they ate for lunch on a blank food pyramid. Next to each group in the pyramid, they wrote down the number of servings they ate from it. On the first day and the two subsequent ones, each child counted out the number of pennies equal to his number of servings for a particular group (three servings of grain equaled three pennies) and put those pennies in that food group's communal cup. The class then counted out the pennies in each of the cups and created a bar graph. The height of each bar corresponded to the number of pennies for that food group. A teacher wrote,

> The students were riveted each time we counted up the pennies in the cup and created the bar graph to represent the servings. There was suspense about how high the count would go, and how tall the bar would be on the graph. The graph was based on information about them and food decisions they had just made. . . . The students were so attached to the graphs that a number of them asked if they could take home the graphs at the end of the year.

The kindergartners' interest spilled over into their daily lives. At lunch, many became more receptive to trying food served at the school. They sometimes even asked for seconds.

About the only sensory area the teachers didn't involve was motor planning, and if they had thought about it, they could have come up with something special there too. All the others—hearing, seeing, taste, smell, touch—were a major part of the experience, as were reading, oral expression, printing, math, science, and art expression: the whole enchilada, so to speak. Through these senses and exercises, the children became comfortable with and informed about food. Most important, they became emotionally interested. It was about what they themselves knew, what they thought, and what they decided, based on their own experiences.

When the time came for the food pyramid to be replaced by other educational materials, the kids felt as though they had lost a friend.

READING LABELS

But the teachers weren't done. The next stage was to introduce the children to the food labels on packages. Once the children realized that most food packages had labels with nutritional values, they avidly compared the numbers.

For this part of the project, children broke into small teams and compared the labels of six packages collected from school snacks and foods typically eaten at home. They looked at the amount of sugar, protein, and sodium and picked out which foods had the most and which had the least of these ingredients. The class shared their results, and the children quickly realized the perfect food with just the right amounts of everything was difficult to find. As an additional math challenge, they pooled all the labels from the teams and sorted the labels from most to least of each of these three ingredients.

The children put this newfound tool to use. They lectured their parents on healthy eating habits and checked the labels at home. They admonished teachers about eating popcorn with too much butter. They checked the labels on school snacks and lunch items and decided which were the healthiest. This sleuthing had a profound effect. Some children chose not to drink chocolate milk or eat ice cream because of the fat content and threw out pretzels that were too salty. One child reacted with glee upon discovering that Italian ice had zero grams of fat.

One interesting food fact they came upon when reading labels was that Total cereal is fortified with a high percentage of iron. A science experiment in the making—could the iron be separated from the cereal? The children crushed some Total in a bowl and stirred in some water using a magnet. To everyone's surprise, after a bit of swishing, they could see a build-up of iron on the magnet. Needless to say, they couldn't wait to tell their parents and friends.

The teachers had the children summarize their new knowledge in two productions: one a book and one a play. To produce a special classroom food book, each child was in charge of one page on which he wrote (with the help of the teacher) about a favorite food fact and illustrated the information. It was all based on the children's expertise. With its own place on the classroom's bookshelf, the book became a part of the permanent resources on nutrition.

The class performance at the end of the year was called "The Trouble with Treats: A Troll's Tale" (a loose adaptation of *Three Billy Goats Gruff*). The performance had a plot full of nutrition facts, high drama provided by an intervention of the "food police," a narrator who was thrilled to explain the food pyramid to the audience, and actors whose lines let them share their new knowledge with the other schoolchildren—telling them what was perhaps even better than an ice cream sundae, or at least most of the time.

When the teachers put the children's food pyramid back on the wall at the end of the school year, one child walked into the room and, sighing with pleasure, said, "It feels GOOD to see the food pyramid up again."

Whether he now ate onions, mushrooms, or—geez—eggplant is not known, but he certainly cared about what he ate and felt the power of his own knowledge to make good decisions for himself.

15

Helping Sally
Strengthening the Trunk and the Roots

The chapters in Parts Two and Three have offered a lot of information—enough so that a process to pull it all together might be helpful to some readers. Enter Sally, the nine-year-old from Chapter 1 who had a reading comprehension problem. We will use her story to show how her parents can use the descriptions and questions about the thinking levels and the sensory information to create a profile of her learning strengths and weaknesses. Please return to Chapter 1 and reread the first couple of pages (up to "Examining Sally's Problems") to refresh your memory.

WHAT SALLY'S PARENTS SAW

Sally's parents knew from their own observations that she was a sweet, good-natured girl who had stresses at school, some of which she handled fairly well and some not so well. They were acutely aware of her reading problem and knew how much it bothered her. This was the target of their efforts. They also knew she had coordination problems, but that didn't really worry them. Mom had some of the same issues, and she had made it through life all right so far. Sally's worries about the cool girls at school were a bit of a concern too, but their chats with other parents affirmed that many kids have these feelings about classmates at school. So what could they learn from thinking about Sally's problems through the lens of the Learning Tree?

The Thinking Levels

1. Attention: They knew that she didn't have any trouble paying attention, except maybe when she was nervous.

2. Engagement: She was warm and friendly and liked being involved with other people.

3. Interaction and Communication: This gave her parents pause. They realized that sometimes Sally could get confused and misinterpret their expressions. It seemed as though she had not quite mastered the full range of emotions that gestures convey. However, she could carry on a good conversation and was able to initiate appropriate expressions and gestures.

4. Problem-Solving: Again, a little mixed message here. Sally didn't have any trouble letting her needs be known, but she did have trouble with following directions. It depended on how complex they were.

5. Using Ideas Meaningfully: Mom had certainly talked enough with Sally about her problems at school to know that Sally could answer questions about her upset feelings. Mom hadn't paid that much attention to the other emotions, but she thought Sally was okay. Sally clearly could offer meaningful ideas and opinions and liked playing with peers.

6. Logical Thinking: Mom could see that Sally had little lapses here. Sometimes when Sally was unhappy about school and Mom didn't take as much time to comfort her, Sally would become upset with her but not really be able to explain why. Also, with fairly complex stories that required adding in an imaginative piece, Sally had more trouble compared to her friends. Her old friendships went along pretty well, but with new acquaintances, she had trouble reading their signals (just like she had trouble reading words), so her logic in understanding if they liked her or not broke down. Even though she was warm and sweet, new friendships were more difficult because she was unsure of herself here.

7. Multicausal Thinking: Here her parents started to see bigger lapses. Although Sally could give multiple reasons for her likes and dislikes and sometimes could understand multiple reasons for another's actions, she did think in terms of all or nothing when looking at her own problems. She couldn't give more than one reason for her reading problems. For her, a bad reading day boiled down to her being "the dumbest girl in the class."

8. Comparative and Gray-Area Thinking: Sally often talked about liking some friends better than others. She made comparisons when choosing what to buy at the store. She certainly had the idea of thinking at this level and of seeing shades of gray. But, again, her all-or-nothing thinking about herself at times of stress made it clear that she couldn't maintain this level evenly.

9. Reflective Thinking: Sally was a little young to be expected to have a firm footing at this level, but her abilities were budding. She could reflect on friendships somewhat. At times when she couldn't quite read the motives of others, she didn't assume they disliked her or that she was unpopular. She was simply confused about what they meant. This changed when she judged herself in the context of her reading problems. Then she assumed that the other kids probably laughed at her and thought she was dumb. She lost the ability to appreciate her talents while acknowledging that she had some areas that needed improving, just like most people have.

Mom and Dad described a young girl who did fine at the beginning levels and had strengths in her warmth, her ability to hold a conversation and offer opinions, and her understanding of some of her feelings. She had, in fact, some strength at every level, but as she progressed up the levels, her weaknesses became more obvious. Looking at each sense helped her parents see how she could broaden the range of her thinking levels and use her strengths to improve her reading.

The Senses

1. Auditory Processing: Her parents remembered that Sally learned to talk fairly easily and initially made the appropriate sounds, "Ma Ma," "Da Da," as well as any tot. She also liked to be read to as a child and look at the pictures, but when she began to read, she stumbled on words (the more syllables, the worse it was) and couldn't really describe the story afterward. Her rendition never made the parts of the story fit together to get to the conclusion. It became more bewildered the longer she tried to explain. Things just didn't stay in order. Her parents could see how this went along with her inability to follow the instructions for doing homework. And they could see that her stress over the situation only made it worse.

2. Motor Planning and Sequencing: This was an easy one. Sally had problems with her gross motor planning and sequencing, whether in PE or in trying to do sports or dance. It gave her almost as much stress as reading. Even though they didn't put much value on this skill, Sally's parents started to appreciate that her problems with moving in a certain sequence resembled her problems with sequencing a story.

This was not so with her fine motor skills. Sally was quite a nice artist and took much pleasure from this talent.

3. Regulation: Sally had mild regulatory problems, mainly being a little hypersensitive to noise. It made her somewhat unsettled and anxious so that any problems she had with sequencing or reading— either words or people's reactions—were more difficult for her. She complained to her parents about getting funny feelings (overwhelmed) when the playground was really noisy and hectic or when a group activity was loud. Most of the time she could keep herself settled down. She just didn't like it.

4. Visual-Spatial Processing: Here Sally excelled. She was the navigator for Mom. She knew where she was and took security from that knowledge. This strength merged with her artistic one. She not only portrayed images accurately but she also created and composed interesting scenes.

Because anxiety is part of Sally's profile, let's just say a few things about it before describing what Sally's parents can do to help her.

Anxiety

Just as happiness, sadness, and excitement are normal, healthy feelings and part of growing up, feelings such as anxiety can become a challenge, particularly if they disrupt one's abilities. Adults may find adaptive ways to manage and reduce anxiety. But children, swimming in this new feeling, experience it merely as life as they know it. They often don't even have a word to identify it or a hint they can do something about it. Sometimes the anxiety is specifically because of the learning problem—for example, Sally's feelings about reading in class; sometimes it's more global. Then an existing learning problem is frequently affected indirectly. Let's look at what happens when the anxiety is because of a learning problem.

Children typically get anxious when they feel uncertain about their ability to do a task, be it completing math problems, essays, or complex directions. To cope with this uncertainty—whether because of weak fine motor or visual-spatial skills or a language challenge or any other challenge that interferes—they are likely to develop an escape route. They may cope by avoiding, by becoming aggressive, by withdrawing, or by feeling inadequate. Avoiding the task entirely (they don't have homework, they are too sick to go to school); getting negative or oppositional ("I'm not going to do it!"); and being depressed and feeling down on oneself, or semi-living in a fantasy world and not dealing with the reality of doing the task are time-proven reactions. If a child has a learning problem, it often becomes worse when she is anxious.

Anxiety makes us all more literal and concrete—harder to be reflective and to concentrate—even if we have devised a clever escape route. It's nearly impossible to block out anxiety completely. The levels of thinking we have achieved come under stress and, not surprisingly, can become a little shaky. The three parameters we described earlier—reaching a level, giving it breadth and range, and stabilizing it—all come under attack. Depending on the stress, some children fall apart more than others.

In Sally's case, she didn't try to block out the anxiety, but her response did make her level of thinking less stable. With the reading problem, she lost the ability in that one area to use the three highest levels of thinking (multicausal, comparative/gray-area, reflective) to help her keep the problem in perspective and solve it. She immediately reduced her abilities to all or nothing.

HOW HER PARENTS HELPED SALLY

The discussion in Chapter 1 of a plan for helping Sally details three areas: reflective thinking, auditory processing and sequencing, and sensory overreaction. Now that Part Two has described more specific exercises and activities, we can expand on these ideas. We also offer some suggestions for dealing with anxiety.

1. Strengthening Sally's reflective thinking skills: Supporting this level starts with helping Sally practice the lower ones of multicausal and the comparative/gray-area thinking. Firming up those will give Sally a more stable foundation for this final thinking level. Sally's parents have many opportunities during daily chitchats with her to encourage her to express opinions using the multicausal and comparative/gray-area levels. Initiating discussions on topics that are already comfortable for her will help her to feel secure in this thinking. Then she can gradually move into less comfortable areas.

Two obvious areas that meet this definition for Sally are her strengths in drawing and visual-spatial skills. When Sally shows her parents her artwork and they admire it, they can ask her an assortment of questions that let her feel their support, interest, and admiration. Through the questions, they can let her be the boss through her showing them how she does things. Basically, this is Floortime with an older child. They need to enter her world, follow her lead, and provide supportive challenges so that she takes charge. When children get to be the boss, their enthusiasm pulls them along to expand their thinking. For instance, let's say that she has created several drawings that use different color schemes. Her parents can ask her to demonstrate what she did so that they can learn how to do it. They can use the moment to practice comparative thinking by asking about which drawing she likes best and why, then second-best, and so on. When she sees how nice her drawings are, how does it make her feel? The same can be applied to her visual-spatial skills. Take an example when she is able to find something in the house that is lost, perhaps the TV remote. After being sincerely appreciative, they can ask her to show them and explain what she does so that they can be better searchers. Why did she look in a certain place? How did she think of that? She becomes the teacher. Explaining something that has interest and emotional value to her will improve her sequencing skills without her even realizing it.

As she becomes more secure in being logical with these topics and more able to judge gradations in things she has done, she can gradually move into talking about skills, such as reading and movement, where she feels much less secure. But first she needs to strengthen these core abilities in areas where she can already reflect more broadly on her abilities while maintaining her thinking levels.

2. Strengthening her auditory processing and sequencing: Sally had a few skills to work on in this sensory mode. She needed to be able to connect visual images to sounds, keep the sequence of the sounds in mind, and improve her overall sequencing of directions. First, Sally can use the same exercises as Isabelle, the singer with sight-reading problems in Chapter 9. The main problem for both was in converting what they saw into what they heard, although Isabelle's strong sense was auditory and Sally's was visual-spatial. In these exercises, Sally's parents needed to start at a level that she could do correctly 70–80 percent of the time and after a little practice make it slightly more challenging.

As for Sally's reading comprehension, her parents had to find a way to encourage her to practice something she found upsetting. Sally's artistic abilities were the perfect approach. Her parents suggested that she choose a book that she enjoyed reading. Then they played a game. Sally would read the story and then draw it. Her parents would guess what the story was about from the pictures Sally drew. Sally could have acted out the story as well, but she preferred drawing it. Using her artistic and visual abilities, Sally was able to begin to see how the different parts of stories relate. Gradually the stories that she read and understood became more complex because of her growing security in following the narrative arc. Her ability to pronounce written words smoothly also kept up with the sophistication of the story because of her exercises on integrating auditory and visual patterns.

As for sequencing sounds and following directions, here again Sally's strong visual-spatial sense could support her weaker sequencing skills. A treasure hunt is the perfect way to practice following directions, with the added pleasure of inviting friends to join in. With this activity, Sally has the security of her visual-spatial sense to keep her oriented along with the motivation of the treasure to follow the directions. Of course, with any of these exercises, it is a question of how difficult the first try is. Sally just needs to be comfortable with the level; she doesn't have to do it perfectly.

Last, working on her motor planning and sequencing skills can reinforce the improvements gained from the exercises above. Sally may seem a bit too old for the beginning stages of the Evolution Game in Chapter 10, but because Mom has similar problems, they may have fun going back to the first rung and spurring each other on, racing worm against worm or having a friendly crocodile stroll. Otherwise, Sally can pick a stage in evolution that she wants to try and begin to practice. As her coordination, rhythm, balance, and left/right integration progress, she can try other activities, such as pretending to be a ballerina or to play tennis. And when there is a competition with Mom or Dad, Sally gets to win most of the time.

3. Diminishing her sensory overreaction: Sally needs to learn how to identify noisy environments that make her feel uneasy and overwhelmed. Because she already has begun to notice this reaction herself, sympathetic discussions about potential types of situations will help her become more aware. With the awareness will come opportunities to figure out how to reduce the impact of the noise, such as to get out of the middle of it for a short time or to figure out how long she can deal with it before getting bothered. Simply having a sense of control over it will give her some reassurance.

4. Improving her coping with anxiety: Because we have not discussed this before, we want to give a fuller picture than just what Sally needs.

It is surprising how an empathetic listener can help a child feel more secure and capable of dealing with her anxiety. It is all about tuning into her, being empathetic, and hanging out. Adults, who may be equally anxious over their child's problem, often like to find a solution right away. This temptation is to be avoided. Children aren't looking for a solution yet. First, they want to be understood and comforted. Who is to blame or what is to be done are not the first priorities. The more parents are relaxed and patient (infinitely patient is good), the more the child will respond to empathetic overtures.

Sally's parents already encouraged her to talk about how much she hated reading and how she'd cancel reading classes if she were the principal. They let her verbalize her feelings of frustration and anger at those who were making her do things that are so hard—them, her teachers, her tutor—as well as her feelings of sadness, incompetence, or confusion. The best antidote to these feelings is for parents or teachers to listen with compassion. At this point, there's no need to present the reasons why reading is so important, just a need to help separate out the different feelings and fantasies that are associated with the anxiety. There's "I'm going to fail," or "I can't think straight," or, "I'll look like an idiot." One child told me, "My brain just doesn't work, and I'm afraid that it'll never work again." Verbalizing these fears to an empathetic, understanding adult can decrease the anxiety.

For children who use escape routes (which Sally didn't), parents need to help identify them in a gentle manner so that they become comfortable in acknowledging them. Again, this starts with the listener being empathetic. After a child is very comfortable in identifying situations that bring out the ostrich or tigress or whatever, then parents can comment in a lighter tone, asking in such a way that the child gets to decide if she was or wasn't escaping. If a child copes by avoiding, a parent can say, "Oh! Is that the ostrich—sticking her head in the sand?" Once the child can talk easily about being an ostrich, a little tease can help take the edge off so that the child can admit, "I'm being an ostrich right now because I really don't want to do this." Or "No, I'm not being an ostrich. I'm just not interested in doing that." If she learns how to be aware of fears rather than fight them, she will relax more and approach the learning problem and the anxiety surrounding it as a challenge to solve, not a fear to avoid.

There are also specific relaxation tools, such as learning to breathe slowly and deeply or simply to take a thirty-second break to stop the escalation of feelings. Taking a break from a task and then gradually coming back to it lets a child back off the anxiety and build up her skills in a low-pressure environment. The "Tomorrow Game" is another one. The problem situation is about to arise in school—Sally has to read a poem aloud in class the next day. Anticipating the situation, talking through all the feelings, identifying reactions, and working out a plan can make the event much less threatening for her. The intensity of the fears and fantasies, once they are acknowledged, usually decreases. Sally's plan could include drawing out the poem's characters and actions at home beforehand so that she has a visual sense of the meaning that in-creases her feelings of security.

Parents can practice these techniques with their child to see which are the most helpful.

Last, children need extra practice in the trouble spot. The chapters in this section are filled with exercises to bolster a particular weakness—whether through going way back to the basics in the sensory development pathway or practicing the actual skill, such as Jack (in Chapter 9) did when learning to answer more complex essay questions. Obviously, the more children improve, the less anxious and overwhelmed they feel. Sometimes extra practice is hard to come by because another problem interferes. For example, the child who struggles with writing essays but also struggles with fine motor skills. Don't let her fine motor challenges hold back her essay-writing. Instead, as we suggest in Chapter 18, give her a tape recorder so that she can get her thoughts down. If someone types it, the majority of the writing is done. She can then work on the essay to improve it. While she is building up her fine motor skills, she still has the ability to practice organizing her thoughts and making her point.

Typically, children who have trouble sequencing information (whether auditory, visual, or motor) get more fragmented, disorganized, and anxious. Sally is a perfect example of this. A timed test just makes the situation more stressful. For children with processing problems, we often recommend untimed tests because intelligence has nothing to do with speed. The same goes for untimed essays. Anxiety can jumble up exam questions very quickly. Some tasks in life require speed; most don't. The really important academic ones require unhurried reflective thinking.

All parents can work out their own way of supporting their children and decreasing their anxiety. The important ingredients are to empathize with the feelings, help them to identify their escape routes, suggest fun activities to strengthen the weaker skill gradually (they need 70 to 80 percent mastery), work with teachers to lessen the load in the challenging area, and work on strengths so children have a balanced view of themselves. Over time, as children become more flexible and stable in their thinking abilities, they will learn to handle anxiety and not let it undermine their growth and development.

PART FOUR
THE BRANCHES

16

The Learning Tree in Action
The Sidwell Friends Dinosaur Project

By Richard Lodish, Ed.D., with Marion Dowling

Mystery and discovery ignite the curiosity of any kid. And what is more mysterious and exciting than dinosaurs?

A group of five- and six-year-old kindergarteners at Sidwell Friends School had an experience in learning that they would remember for a long time. Launched into a full-scale investigation of the age of dinosaurs, they avidly researched the facts, developed theories, and used their imaginations. Here is how the program, designed and led by teacher Marion Dowling, worked.

To attract and engage the children from the start, the teachers transformed the classroom into an interactive dinosaur encounter and let the kids live and breathe dinosaurs for about six weeks. The kids read books about dinosaurs, looked at dinosaur posters that covered the walls, touched and explored dinosaur fossils that lay about, and designed homes for dinosaurs (after doing research into dinosaur habitat). They learned about the ferocious and powerful ones and the weaker and smaller ones. They built thrones for the powerful ones; they constructed a safe habitat for the weaker ones. The wall chart listed the dinosaurs, smallest through largest, with all the details: name, meaning of the name, height, weight, and length. Sequencing a multitude of ideas, the children learned to differentiate between the types and to see how certain patterns—such as where they lived, what they ate, and what physical traits they had—pertained to certain groups.

Dinosaurs are pretty exciting to kids. But it isn't just the known facts that pull them in. It's the mystery. When it comes to dinosaurs, no one knows all the answers—not teachers, not parents, and not older students. Any child can come up with a theory. The space for thinking and imagination is endless as children delve into a lost world. As budding scientists and explorers, they have some facts, but they can also use these facts to develop their own ideas of how things might have been. As one of their teachers said,

> It is clear that the catalyst for the children's enthusiasm emerges from their belief that teachers and students are truly learning and investigating together. Children eagerly listen to the hypotheses and theories that others hold. Careful attention and a communal sense of awe and wonder typically mark the class discussions.

The teachers begin with a simple question: "Have you ever seen a dinosaur?" In their initial response, children enthusiastically raise their hands to share stories about museums, books, and movies, but ultimately one child utters the "E" word—extinction. Some don't really know what it means because it is a difficult concept for young children. But the teachers tell them that dinosaurs have not existed for 65 million years and that no one really knows why they all died. The class works together to hash out the meaning of extinction until there is an agreed-upon definition that suits everyone.

The children become a "collective group of truth seekers and mystery solvers." To do this, they use all the levels of thinking, even verging into the advanced ones of abstraction and reflection.

One or two children always know the meteorite theory and eagerly enlighten their fellow students during the discussion of extinction: "A meteorite hit the Earth!" Rather than ending the conversation, this leads to the next question: "How could a meteorite kill so many thousands of dinosaurs?" A trip to the sandbox to drop a rock in the sand gives them a hint. They see the dust and the dirt fly up and listen to the teachers explain one theory—that if the dirt stays up in the air, it will block the sunlight and cool the air, causing plants to die and leaving the plant eaters with nothing to eat. With this theory as a starter, the children eagerly share their own ideas. The culmination of this part becomes page one in their individual research books. Each child draws a picture about dinosaurs and after finishing, dictates to the teacher his own theory of the dinosaurs' extinction.

The following week brings another question: "How do we know what dinosaurs looked like?" Discussions about what is and isn't known lead the children to look to the animals of today, such as elephants and giraffes but especially reptiles because dinosaurs are in the reptile family. Page two of their research book becomes their own version of what dinosaurs looked like.

Dinosaurs with particular body parts—such as the stegosaurus with plates; the triceratops with horns and frill; the newly discovered long-neck whose neck was twice its body length; and T. rex with puny arms, big teeth, and a two-legged gait—collectively get a week because each of these traits lend themselves to the development of theories for why. Multicausal thinking abounds. To understand how tall T. rex really was, the children stand next to a telephone pole. To get a sense of the height of the tallest dinosaur, they make a trip to a parking garage and ride the elevator to the fourth floor. They measure and compare.

The children even make recess part of the project. They play dinosaurs, and because dinosaurs didn't talk, all they can do is roar and gesture. The powerful ones sometimes are kind and other times ferocious; the small ones who are slighter but fast solve their problems using those strengths. The same action takes place in the sandbox where dinosaurs made by the children battle each other to determine the king of the sand hill.

The art teacher supplies clay to make dinosaurs and crayons for drawings, the science teacher talks about dinosaur bones and fossils, the kindergarten teachers provide time for discussion and picture books and posters. The finale is a special trip to the natural history museum, where in groups of two children with an adult, they reconstruct all the information from the past weeks. They look at the models in the museum and draw what they find to be the most interesting characteristics. Back at school, they have dinosaur cookies waiting for them.

In this dynamic learning environment, children were encouraged to imagine dinosaurs, to think logically about them, and to form theories and understand such abstract ideas as extinction. They discussed their own ideas and listened to others. Everything was multidisciplinary, all the senses contributed, and the children were able to get as close to the answers as any good scientist could.

Success is easy when children want to be involved in what they are learning. This is true for all children, but as we have said, interest is particularly important for children with learning disabilities because they need extra excitement to push through the difficult parts. Cooperating and collaborating in school, learning from someone else's strengths, helping out with another's weaknesses, and sharing what they know allow children to feel good about themselves.

Dorothy Llittell Greco

17

Reading Comprehension

In the previous chapters, we portrayed children with reading comprehension problems. Sally was the first. Her reading problem started out with the basics—differentiating sounds, which led to not being able to hold the sound sequences in order, which led to general sequencing problems. Jack also had problems with sequencing. His difficulty showed up with confusion over understanding complex questions. And then there was Eric, who needed more experiences to understand the concepts he read and wrote about. Jack's and Eric's problems emerged mainly in their writing, but the problems actually stemmed from a lack of comprehension.

Another problem that can interfere with reading comprehension is the child's inability to connect to another person's ideas.

SOPHIE'S STORY

Sounding out and reading words were not a problem for Sophie. When she read aloud in class, her delivery was as fluid as any of the other children. Her problem was more complex: she couldn't explain what she had read. Even a couple of simple sentences—"Mary loved her new baby doll. She took her to the park. At night, she gave her a big kiss and put her to bed"—confused her. When the teacher asked her about what Mary did and how Mary might have felt, Sophie froze and said nothing. She couldn't answer the question. The teacher recommended help for Sophie. Sophie's parents brought her to see me.

In my office, Sophie was very sweet and eager, but I saw that she didn't respond very much. She expressed her ideas and played creatively—making up little stories about her dolls having lunch or going on an adventure—but when I said, "Sophie, why is your dolly running?" she ignored my question and went on with her story. According to her parents, she often did not respond to what was said at home or school. They thought that along with a reading comprehension problem she may have ADD or ADHD.

I saw a more fundamental problem. Sophie had never learned to fully connect her ideas to those of other people. She never mastered logical thinking. When asked, "Why do you want to wear your parka outside?" Sophie just didn't answer most of the time. Why questions, which call for a logical answer, stymied her.

The full evaluation showed that it was hard for Sophie to process—to take in and comprehend—what other people were saying. It was much easier for her to chatter on her own. Long, two-way conversations and a lot of one-on-one play at home made up the core of my program for Sophie.

To start, her parents gave her incentives to respond to them. When she asked for something, they expressed curiosity about why. They pulled her in by using what had the most emotional appeal to her. "Can I have some yogurt?" "Of course, what flavor is your favorite?" If Sophie answered, it was easy for them to ask why. If she didn't, they pumped up the energy—vocalizing more strongly or becoming more visibly dramatic—to capture her: "Oh, Sophie, strawberry? Or is it lemon?" Gentle, curious, and wooing questions were used.

Little by little, their efforts became more sophisticated. If Sophie didn't give a coherent reason for wanting to go to the playground or a friend's house, they used body language and expression for some of her favorite activities—swinging, hanging from the bars, or playing hopscotch—to pull her into the scene. They enticed her to choose a reason and tell them with words. These tactics helped harness all of Sophie's senses and her motor system into emotionally meaningful exchanges that connected her ideas with theirs. Through practicing, Sophie slowly went from responding coherently only 30 percent of the time, to 50 percent, and finally to 80–90 percent.

Reading comprehension means paying attention and understanding ideas that come from someone else. Making logical connections was essential if Sophie was to comprehend what she and others read in class. For Sophie, as these connections improved, so did her reading comprehension. Paying attention is always the first step in thinking. But simply giving Sophie a label of ADD or ADHD would never have solved her reading problem.

For Sophie to turn around her problem with reading comprehension, you can see how important it was to identify the right missing piece in her development—connecting to the thoughts of others more generally—and for her parents to use her own interests to spark initial connections with them. Interestingly, later on, Sophie developed a hobby that merged her natural gift for telling stories and her acquired strength in reading. She became a storyteller. She drew her stories from old letters, using real lives to weave a drama that kindled an emotional connection with her audience.

BUILDING READING COMPREHENSION

Chapters 8 and 9 outline the auditory roots of reading—from distinguishing different sounds, to associating a sound with its visual representation, and eventually to stringing letters together in order to say the word and to understand what it means. These are the precursors to reading comprehension.

Along with these basic reading skills (roots) go the basic thinking skills (trunk). You can't comprehend beyond the level at which you think. Building on the work of various colleagues, we've come up with a multistep approach to reading comprehension that incorporates all the thinking levels in our tree trunk. Here's a paragraph on each one.

The first step is attending to what is read. As we described in Chapter 8, once a child is able to read sentences and little paragraphs, we want her to make the process a multisensory experience by absorbing the big picture and the details through all her senses and thinking levels. So, the first step in reading comprehension is the first stage in our ability to think: paying attention. You can read the passage along with your child and then being curious, ask her to describe as richly and fully as possible everything there is to see, hear, smell, even taste, including things that aren't stated but the child can guess about. If the scene is simple—such as, "The tree is blowing in the wind"—what does that look like? Does the tree have leaves? Is the wind soft or strong? Do the leaves make a sound in the wind? If the story is more involved, say, about a girl at the zoo, what is happening? What does the girl do? Even if the passage doesn't say what she smells, what does the child think the girl can smell? What color fur do the animals have? What would the fur feel like? How big or small are the animals? What kind of noises do they make? Are the monkeys swinging on branches? Maybe the child can even imitate the movements of the animals in the passage.

Next, it is important to have a child engage in the world. To help the child engage with the reading, you might ask, Is there more than one person in the passage? If so, what's the relationship between the characters? Are there characters "offstage" who are important? (i.e., if a boy in the story thinks he might get a bicycle for Christmas, who might give it to him?) Or is the main character involved with an object (such as a kite or a stuffed animal) or a pet?

A next step involves interaction and communication. Getting the child to think about the emotions and interactions in her reading will also deepen her comprehension. Are there conversations between the characters? Does the girl at the zoo call to her favorite animal so it comes to the fence? How does she feel if it does? What if she wants to stay, and her father thinks it's time to leave? What does the boy say about his new bicycle? Are the others envious?

Next, you and your child can engage in shared problem-solving. Stories are full of problems to be solved. You two can talk about the dilemmas facing the characters and how they can solve them. If the little boy with the new bike is having trouble reaching the pedals, what does he need to do to fix things so he can try it out? Who might help him? Will they need tools? If two little monkeys at the zoo are chasing each other, what can one of them do to get away from the other? What does your child think their mom thinks about it?

At this point, we want to encourage the meaningful use of ideas, to enter the child's realm of imagination. We want to see if the child can embellish the story with some creativity. What might happen next? What might have happened before? Would she change something in the scene? Perhaps the zookeeper would let the girl feed the giraffe. In other words, can the child use her own ideas to add to the passage? Ask plenty of questions so that the child makes sense while elaborating on the tale.

Using logical thinking and connecting ideas together lets the child get to a new level of describing cause and effect. Is anything making the narrator or another character in the passage feel a certain way? Or, even if it's just a story about a tree, how would a tree feel in a storm? The child might answer, "Well, it's snowing so the tree is probably feeling cold, and it's probably not feeling very good." Or "The tree is lonely because there aren't any other trees around." Help the child find any causal relationships that might be implied in the passage.

At a later stage, that of more sophisticated interpretation, a child can apply multicausal, comparative, and gray-area thinking to her reading. Are there many reasons for what happened in the reading passage? Explore many possible feelings and many possible outcomes. Ask the child to compare the characters and the strength of their motivations. For instance, how do the girl's feelings about wanting to stay at the zoo compare to the daddy's feelings about wanting to go home?

An older child who is becoming reflective can evaluate her reading. With a nine- to twelve-year-old, you could ask, "What do you think about that passage?" "What do you think the author was trying to say?" "Did you believe what the characters said?" or "How would you tell the story differently?" Eventually children can begin to apply reflective, critical, and analytical thought to their reading, comparing each passage to other writing and to their own experiences and preferences. They become able to project themselves into the story: "Would you be as upset if the same thing happened to you?" Encourage your child to interpret her reading in terms of similar experiences or different experiences she has had. In other words, Would I want to be like the boy in the story? What about the other characters? What would I do if I were in that situation? Once the child can do this, she will understand the passage and make it a part of herself; then it will be easy for her to remember and explain the text.

Children's ultimate level of comprehension will be determined by their thinking ability because once any information is "uploaded," so to speak, what matters is how it's put together in the mind. As children use higher thinking levels and comprehend more, the passages come alive for them. In their heads, even without thinking about it, good readers see the characters, hear their voices, have a strong sense of them as people, have feelings about them—good ones and bad ones—and understand their struggles. Moving through the levels of thinking helps to make reading passages part of the child's personal experience. That's one of the big differences between just memorizing some facts from a passage and really comprehending the author's main message.

ADDITIONAL READING CHALLENGES

Children can have a variety of other problems that distract them from understanding what they read.

Visual Sensitivities

Some children are so visually sensitive (i.e., hypersensitive) that looking at a white page covered with black letters overwhelms them. They can't discriminate the words. For some children, using their finger to track words on the page keeps them focused, but for others, this natural tool is too difficult. Researchers at MIT have found two innovative techniques for this problem. The first is to take a piece of cardboard and cut out a rectangle just large enough to isolate a word, phrase, or sentence from the rest of the page so that the child focuses on only what's inside the rectangle. Trial and error, based on how much the child can take in at once, will determine the best size for the rectangle. The size of the rectangle can increase as the child gets better at focusing. Eventually, the child will read without the help of the "reading rectangle."

The second technique for children who are visually hypersensitive involves using a blue-tinted piece of plastic to decrease the contrast between the black lettering and the white page. Softening the contrast with a piece of tinted plastic makes it easier for the children to focus on the words and their meaning.

Some children are hyposensitive, which means that the words on the page don't stand out enough. A few tools are available: a yellow-tinted filter that sharpens the contrast between the letter and the paper, larger lettering than usual, a change in the color or style of the lettering, or a change in the color of the paper. Experimenting with these different factors can determine what works for a particular child. Generally, as your child improves and becomes more confident, she won't need to rely on these tools to control either hyper- or hyposensitivity.

Motor System Problems

Another reading challenge we sometimes see is a motor system problem—that is, tracking the text across the page. Some children have difficulty moving their eyes smoothly from left to right or right to left, and they lose the line easily. In this case, in addition to using the rectangular cutout in a piece of cardboard or teaching the child to move a finger under the line of text to guide her eyes, we can also work directly on her visual tracking. One of the best ways is by playing catch with the child. Start by standing close to the child and throwing big Nerf balls, then gradually move farther away and use a smaller ball. This gives the child practice in coordinating eye and hand movements.

Harry Wachs, whom we mentioned before, has a good exercise for strengthening visual tracking. First, hang a pendant with a hole in it on a string and have the child put a pencil into the hole. Next, slowly move the string back and forth so the pendant becomes a pendulum. The goal is for the child to insert the pencil into the hole while the pendulum is swinging, which requires tracking and coordinating eyes and hands. Any game in which the child has to coordinate seeing and doing, such as hitting a moving object, kicking a ball, or playing fast card games like Spit, will improve the child's tracking abilities.

Such a multisensory approach to reading recognizes individual differences in sensory reactivity, sensory processing, and the way we plan our actions. You can experiment to find what works best for your child; however, do this only if you have identified that the child has specific sensory difficulties. For all children with comprehension problems, begin with determining how easy it is for the child, first, to make the connection between the sound and the letter or the word and whether she needs more basic work on that. Next, determine how well the child actually perceives letters and combinations of letters. Then, look at whether the child has an attention problem or a memory challenge. Finally, look at whether the child has trouble comprehending or making inferences beyond the facts, in which case, the challenge comes down to improving the fundamental thinking level.

JULIE'S STORY

As a summary of steps that integrate all levels of thinking into comprehending the written and spoken word, the following is an example based on a formal program, the Affect-Based Language Curriculum (ABLC), developed by colleague Diane Lewis and me. This program successively incorporates work on each level of thinking into improving reading and writing skills.

For her science homework, Julie had to read Ben Franklin's description of his kite experiment and to learn how he proved that lightning was electricity—and she didn't understand it. In an October 19, 1752, letter to Peter Collinson, Franklin had written:

> Make a small cross of two light strips of cedar, the arms so long as to reach to the four corners of a large thin silk handkerchief when extended; tie the corners of the handkerchief to the extremities of the cross, so you have the body of a kite; which being properly

accommodated with a tail, loop, and string, will rise in the air, like those made of paper; but this being of silk is fitter to bear the wet and wind of a thunder gust without tearing. To the top of the upright stick of the cross is to be fixed a very sharp pointed wire, rising a foot or more above the wood. To the end of the twine, next the key may be fastened. This kite is to be raised when a thundergust appears to be coming on, and the person who holds the string must stand within a door or window, or under some cover, so that the silk ribbon may not be wet; and care must be taken that the twine does not touch the frame of the door or window. As soon as any of the thunder clouds come over the kite, the pointed wire will draw the electric fire from them, and the kite, with all the twine, will be electrified, and the loose filaments of the twine, will stand out every way, and be attracted by an approaching finger. And when the rain has wetted the kite and twine, so that it can conduct the electric fire freely, you will find it stream out plentifully from the key on the approach of your knuckle. At this key the phial may be charged: and from electric fire thus obtained, spirits may be kindled, and all the other electric experiments be performed, which are usually done by the help of a rubbed glass globe or tube, and thereby the sameness of the electric matter with that of lightning completely demonstrated.

Julie asked Dad for help. He began at the levels of attention and engagement by asking Julie what she liked about the experiment. Easy! Flying a kite was neat. When he asked what she didn't like and why, she had an answer for that too. She thought that walking in the field, waiting for the clouds and for something to happen, must have been really boring. For Julie and her father, having a conversation was not a challenge. When Dad advanced to the next level of shared problem-solving, however, Julie had more trouble. What steps did Ben Franklin take to do his experiment? Julie couldn't explain. Using the Socratic method and referring back to the text, Dad helped her identify the reasons for flying a kite, for the material in the key, and for the dry material Franklin held in his hand so he didn't get hurt. Julie reread the passage, and Dad asked her questions until she understood the steps in Franklin's experiment. Then, for fun and to add in imagination, her father suggested they pretend to fly their own kite in a storm and that Julie direct the experiment.

For the same exercise with an older child, who might bristle at the "childish" pretending part, you can encourage understanding and creativity with questions: "What would you do if you were Ben Franklin? What do you think the next step would be?" These kinds of questions encourage the child to discuss the passage logically, to give an opinion supported by the facts.

You can move to a higher level of comparative thinking by comparing Franklin to other inventors the child has learned about, such as Thomas Edison: "Whose discovery do you think is more important—Edison's or Franklin's?" "Which one is more interesting?" and so forth. You can build on the child's answers by asking, "Why more interesting? How much did it change our lives?" Finally, we arrive at reflective thinking: "Well, how would you compare what Ben Franklin did to the experiments you've done?" "Who is more of a role model for you, Ben Franklin or Thomas Edison?"

By going through this process, from the first level of attention and engagement up through reflective thinking, you can harness the entire mental team by bringing in all the senses and make reading comprehension a full learning experience: vision (from the pictures describing what Franklin looked like, what the sky looked like); movement (flying a pretend kite or a real one, of course, not during a storm); sound and words (all the conversation); and emotion (Franklin's feelings when he was successful). In other words, from this one science assignment, the child can create a multisensory experience to bring the passage alive and really comprehend it.

Pat Lindamood's colleague, Nancy Bell, has developed a system called "Visualizing/Verbalizing" in which she helps children visualize what they read, which is one step in the approach that I'm describing here. I like to go beyond visualizing to incorporating action, sound, emotion, texture—even taste if possible. We also want children to apply each of our levels of thinking to what they read. When children do this, they truly master each passage. After being guided through this approach for a while, children begin doing it automatically. They become what I call "thinking-based readers" who bring the text alive for themselves. They automatically see the pattern or the main point of the text; they approach the reading creatively, thinking of alternatives; they think about what they like and don't like in the text, and to what degree, and why; and they compare what the author says to what they themselves think about the world. This kind of reading can occur with any text—from a novel to a chapter in a history book.

Marilyn Nolt

18

Expressing Ideas in Writing and Speaking

Jason's ear-to-ear grin signaled victory. His parents had resisted, but he had finally persuaded them that he deserved new roller blades. At another house down the street, Lila's sideways smirk at her little brother revealed her triumph. After listening to her, her parents blamed him for the gooey fingerprints on the couch. Faced with high stakes, both of these fifth-graders were quite adept at organizing a persuasive argument. At school, however, neither could organize an essay with a clear point of view and supporting examples.

They aren't alone. Many high school and college students who are otherwise gifted can't put together a well-organized essay or verbal report. Adults aren't exempt either. One common remedy, outlining the points of the essay, usually doesn't really do the trick. As you may have guessed, using the thinking levels does.

ROBBIE'S STORY

Robbie was a pretty typical nine-year-old—running off to be with his friends, bargaining to stay up late to see his favorite TV show, and getting into fights with his little brother. And while he was both verbal and athletic, Robbie had a problem with his schoolwork. When his teacher asked him to write a few sentences about his favorite part of the weekend, Robbie would start out appropriately, "I went for a walk with my mother in the park," and after a couple of sentences begin to jump around, "It's still raining," and then, "And I like recess." He had no sense of the point he was trying to make. He simply wrote whatever came to mind. Worried because his school essays were so disjointed, his parents brought him to see me.

In my office, Robbie was quite the opposite. When he told me what was really on his mind, he had absolutely no trouble with a logical explanation. He said that his parents favored his seven-year-old little brother. Whenever he and his brother fought, his parents blamed Robbie, saying, "You're older. You should know better." His brother bothered his toys, but his parents never saw that part. By the time they came to see about the noise, it was just Robbie pushing him. He tried much harder than his brother and did better than he did at everything. His parents only saw the fights.

Robbie's strong feelings about his family offered a perfect opening to help him learn to organize his ideas in school.

First, I asked him to tell me the ways he was better than his brother. He eagerly counted them out: "I can read better, throw and catch better, I don't fuss about eating vegetables, and I don't mess up as much. I'm better in lots of ways." I asked him for an example about messing up. "My brother always causes trouble, like taking my toys and getting us into fights," he said. "But I don't mess with his stuff." I suggested to Robbie that we write an essay about these ideas for his parents and asked him what he wanted his parents to know. "OK," he answered, "I want to talk about how my brother bothers me and how I'm better."

"That's a good start," I encouraged, "What comes next?"

Robbie said, "All the stuff I just told you, why I'm better."

"OK," I proposed, "let's do it again." Clearly pleased with having an audience interested in his problem, he quickly ran through the list.

I took out a sheet of paper and said, "Now let's put it down." I drew a big box on top and labeled it, "The Main Point," and underneath I drew littler boxes for each supporting point. I asked him, "So, what's your main point?"

Delighting in the opportunity, Robbie announced, "I'm better than my brother."

We wrote that in the big box, and then I asked, "Now, what are your examples?" In each of the smaller boxes, Robbie wrote the things he had just told me. Finally, I labeled another box at the bottom of the sheet "Conclusion" and explained to him that here he could repeat his main point again now that he had given his examples to support it. For his conclusion, Robbie wrote, "I'm much, much, much better than my brother," and drew a big smiley face.

"OK," I said. "Let's take another piece of paper and write this out in sentences." Patiently, he constructed an essay repeating the points in the boxes. Punctuation and spelling were a bit of an obstacle, but they weren't the point. He was logical and organized and stayed on track. His essay was very reasonable for a nine-year-old.

After Robbie and I went over the general elements of an essay— that is, always having a main point, supporting your main point with examples, and reaching a conclusion—I asked him if he had something else he liked to talk about. Yes, he did, his favorite TV shows. "All right," I said, "What's your main point?"

He eagerly shouted out, "I love TV." I asked him for examples, and he listed all the shows he loved and why. We then diagrammed it together, and he wrote it out as an essay.

Finally, I asked Robbie to tell me about a topic that he wasn't very interested in. "What would be something your teacher might ask you to write about that you're not interested in at all?"

He answered, "Oh, like what I did over the weekend. Sometimes we don't do anything that is fun, and I don't want to write about that."

So I said, "Well, can you write about how Sunday was boring? Can you write about all the un-fun things you did?"

He said, "Yeah," and we went through the exercise again. Proud of his ideas, Robbie read the essay out loud, completely enjoying the opportunity to list everything he found boring and didn't like and why. What I helped Robbie understand was that no matter the topic—even something dull and dreary—he could find something about it that interested him, even if it was why it didn't interest him.

The diagramming and organizing helped, but they weren't the heart of the effort. The heart of our exercise was his motivation. When he wrote about something that had emotional meaning to him—good or bad—he could write a very nice essay.

A while later, Robbie's history teacher assigned a report to describe the life of settlers 200 years ago. "Yuck," was Robbie's response. That chapter in his history book had mainly showed pictures of the settlers' cabins and tools and described the children's chores. The chapter seemed monotonous to Robbie; the settlers' lives were boring. All those kids did was work, and he was just glad that he didn't live then. He told his mother that he didn't have any ideas to write about. This time Robbie's mom knew what to do.

Nearby there just happened to be a "living" museum that recreated a colonial farm. Standing in a small, smoky log cabin with a dirt floor and little light gave Robbie experiences that his dry history book couldn't. The straw mattresses were rolled up next to the wall; tallow candles, which had just been dipped, hung from the rafter to harden. He saw the root cellar and the crops out the back door where chickens and pigs roamed around. And he discovered that kids back then had toys too: hoops, balls, games, a lot of stuff.

He particularly liked the large metal hoop. With a little practice, he became pretty good at getting it to roll straight by brushing the top with a stick as it went round. When Robbie came home, he quickly figured out his main idea—that kids worked hard but had fun too— and diagrammed the supporting ideas—that they had cool toys, got to help build a fire, could chase the chickens around when parents weren't watching, and didn't have to take a bath very often.

The museum being so close by was lucky, but if that hadn't been the case, his parents could have sparked his ideas and opinions in other ways. A more informative library book could be the basis for imagining a cabin and talking about what it would have been like or, perhaps, a corner of the room could have been set up to resemble the scene Robbie took from the book. Or his parents could simply ask him questions. Why was he glad he didn't live in colonial times? What would he miss? He would be able to develop his first thoughts—that life back then was all work and no play. They took this tack for other topics that he had no interest in, and gradually Robbie came to apply the basic structure to topics that were less emotionally "close to home."

Robbie's problems with essay writing are fairly common. Let's take a look at the key steps in writing an essay and see how they pertain to children of different ages.

HAVING SOMETHING TO SAY

For children to want to share their ideas, they first have to have experiences and opinions. After an exhausting week of carpooling to various activities, you may think that your child has plenty to draw on, but tap dancing, swimming, or basketball, while good for gaining skills, may or may not be emotionally important to the child. Sometimes, to want to write about them, children need experiences that excite them and feel fresh and new.

Take Robbie. He had vivid reactions to his little brother and TV shows, enough so that those two topics meant something to him. He could easily share his feelings and opinions about them. But once he got past those two subjects, his range was limited. Exposure to new situations that he connected to on a personal level was an important part of his developing essay-writing skills.

Some children naturally develop a wide range of ideas; others, whose families engage enthusiastically in many activities, also tend to have a bigger range; still others are just slower and need more encouragement. In any case, a variety of new experiences will boost the range of ideas of all children, even if your child already has a lot of opinions and favorite hobbies and friends.

Hikes in wild areas, the zoo, a bus ride, the supermarket, a beach, a farm, the county fair, a child-friendly museum, a visit to your office, or just a walk in a new part of town—all these can draw your child into a bigger world. He learns new words and, at the same time, builds emotional associations to these words and opinions about what they represent. Your child becomes more aware of different worlds and forms opinions about them. Looking at books together is great too, but smelling a rose or touching a thistle, eating a new kind of food or building a sand castle is more likely to inspire new ideas and new likes and dislikes.

Even on ordinary days, you can ask questions about things your child already enjoys. Ask questions about things he may have not noticed before: when making cookies—why do you think the cookies are all round? At the supermarket, why does the store put cookies and candy near the cash register?

Obviously, the new experiences shouldn't overload the child. Running around from the park to the supermarket to the swimming pool to the zoo to fill up the child's day won't work. His explorations need to be fun but calm enough so that he can enjoy his new words and ideas—so that he can soak up the spirit of his new experiences.

WANTING TO SAY IT

"Wanting to say it" means having a point of view that you wish to share. Too often, when asked about a subject, children merely regurgitate facts. More and more teachers have to "teach to the test," and more and more tests examine knowledge of facts. Introductions to important historical subjects, such as the Declaration of Independence or the Bill of Rights, often mean memorizing the texts with little discussion of their significance. Wars are not seen as battling ideologies but as a list of battles, generals, and dates. Robbie hadn't been asked to form an opinion about the life of early settlers from his schoolwork. An iteration of facts about those times did not help him find a point of view and a desire to express it. Yet, writing a good essay is all about wanting to express a point of view backed up by facts.

Even with the best educators and the most innovative programs, valuing one's own point of view and wanting to express it won't happen if the classroom is the child's first experience with forming opinions. Wanting to say it comes from feeling that one's point of view or ideas about a subject are important and valued. What child wouldn't like to have the floor to expound on why a certain video game is something he has to have or why his favorite fast food hamburger is better than the home-cooked version? You can nurture this attitude in your children, no matter the age, through the simplest of conversations. It's all about taking an interest in what's on your child's mind: to listen carefully; to express interest by commenting, asking a question, or sharing an experience of your own; and to encourage the child to elaborate. Whether tasting pies at the county fair or going to the aquarium, ask your children's opinions about what they do or don't like. And challenge them to back up their opinions with facts or their observations. From around the age of three on, many children can answer why questions and begin to back up their opinions.

Well before essays are assigned, teachers can do the same exercise to encourage opinions and debate. If so, when children advance to their first writing assignment, they will already feel comfortable with having a point of view and expressing it.

Being able to express ideas is a powerful gift. But valuing your child's ideas so that he wants to say it does not mean agreeing with or sanctioning the opinion. Just because a child thinks making bathroom noises in front of company is cool and can give reasons why, you need not allow the behavior. Nonetheless, in a private conversation, you two can discuss it, even taking an interest in the child's version of what's humorous or provocative, for that matter.

EXPRESSING IDEAS LOGICALLY

Once your child has exciting new ideas and wants to share, these ideas float out like a burst of bubbles. Sometimes the enthusiasm and pleasure are palpable. But for a child of any age, you want to ask a most important question: is the child making sense? Are his ideas generally orderly and logical? To answer this, listen for the connections between his ideas. When you and he begin trading ideas back and forth, watch to see if each connection makes sense. Connecting ideas logically is crucial for the continued development of children's ability to make sense of what they see and hear and to express it.

As we've discussed, by around three years of age, children should begin to answer why questions, usually with one simple reason. But what if a child can't answer "why?" What if there are lapses in his circle of ideas, like Robbie's when he tried to write an essay about his weekend? What is going on?

Again, as we've said, emotions organize thoughts. Emotions are central. If anyone—child or adult—thinks without emotional in-volvement, his thoughts will be more random. Children over the age of four who argue about something that's important to them—why they want to go on a picnic with friends or, as in Robbie's case, why they are better than their brother—usually demonstrate impeccable logic. But some exchanges do not involve such strong emotional tugs. So, if your child wanders a bit, the key is creating an emotional involvement with the ideas. Entice some emotion from your child like I did with Robbie when he raised the issue of his brother.

No one—neither child nor adult—can have too much practice at being logical. If your six-year-old really wants something, challenge him to explain why. Encourage debating. That will give him a lot of practice in being logical (and keep you on your toes too). As your child becomes logical and makes sense most of the time, continue to challenge him to give more than one reason for each point he wants to make.

A child who has ideas to talk about and can also present them logically has a good foundation for writing essays and giving oral reports. (These draw on the same basic skills.) The first experience of giving a presentation, in nursery school or kindergarten, is usually show-and-tell. Most of the time, the child is in charge of this traditional rite and chooses which favored object to bring from home. This encourages emotional engagement with the topic and helps the child to stay on track. But within just a couple of years the situation may be less favorable. The second-grade teacher might ask her students to give an oral report about a trip to the museum or the reasons for a national holiday. These moments can be hard for children, especially if the subject doesn't interest them.

Expressing ideas evolves through the different thinking levels—from the basic why level; to the multicausal, comparative, gray-area thinking level; and, finally, the truly reflective thinking level (Chapter 5 gives details on these levels). To give a sense of how these levels of thinking expand, we can follow a child's thoughts about a subject as she gets older. Let's start with Molly as a six-year-old who has had some problems with expressing her ideas.

Molly had to give a school talk on what she did during the summer. First, to help her get interested, her mother asked, "What was the most fun thing you did this summer?" Molly wanted to talk about the beach. "Okay," says Mom, "that is your main subject. So, what made the beach exciting?" Molly talked about seeing dolphins, swimming in the ocean, and going to the boardwalk to ride in bumper cars. Mom suggested she draw the beach, with the dolphins, swimmers, and bumper cars. That would help Molly remember to give examples. Using the drawing, Molly's talk for her class about why the beach was her favorite activity that summer was clear, organized, and logical.

As children move into the seven- to nine-year age range, they get into comparative thinking. When Mom asked her now–third-grader what made the beach exciting that summer, Molly declared, "The beach was more fun this year than last year because I was big enough to go on more rides at the boardwalk." On her own, she was able to compare it to the year before.

Mastering comparative thinking leads into discussions (or arguments) that contain "shades of gray"—for instance, giving several reasons why one thing is better than another with the reasons rated from the most important to the least important. For nine-year-old Molly, this meant that "the beach was much, much better than last year—last year it was a six out of ten, this year it was a nine out of ten." Later on, these kinds of discussions will prove to be good practice for discussing the reasons for historical or fictional events and appreciating subtle levels of difference.

Our journey into advanced levels of expressing ideas doesn't end here. As children progress into the teen years, they move into the realm of reflective thinking. Both in oral and written presentations, they become not only logical and subtle but also able to critically analyze what they write or speak about. As a teenager, Molly had become quite reflective: "I like the beach because I'm an outdoor person—I don't like staying in and playing computer games all summer like some of my friends." Ultimately, Molly could express her reflections in a very sophisticated way. "I love being outside. I get all kinds of ideas there when I explore the dunes and the tide pools. I feel part of the whole ocean world. When I'm older, I plan to live at the beach."

As children advance through these levels of thinking and gradually face more complex subjects to research and write about, they'll be able to fall back on the initial strategy learned in grade school and ask themselves, "What is the main point?" "What am I trying to say?" "What examples do I need to support my main point?" These questions, though seemingly simple, are the basis for constructing a good essay at any time.

An important secondary issue is, "Does this idea really belong? Or is it just an idea that I think is interesting?" People are reluctant to give up interesting thoughts, even if they are unrelated to their main point. With a young child, you might hear him argue why he deserves an ice-cream cone by describing why some flavors taste better than others. But this idea doesn't really support his argument. A child who is drawing a picture to plan a talk can put these ideas on another sheet of paper. Once he is able to diagram an essay with words, these interesting ideas can be put aside on another page or side column, separate from the essay itself. A parent or teacher might suggest, "That's very interesting and may be something you want to write about sometime. Why don't you put it down here, on this other page, as an additional idea?" The child learns to discriminate between points that are essential and points that are not.

CREATIVE WRITING

Creative writing may seem like a different creature than essay writing, yet it follows the same structure, just in a more subtle way. A story has a plot with character development and incidents that all contribute to the plot. Novels usually have themes, with each character representing and embellishing a different aspect of a theme. Various elements of the novel reflect aspects of the theme. Some novelists create a structure unconsciously; others diagram the intricacies of the plot. Although the diagram may evolve, novelists usually have a visual map of the narrative in their minds as they write. Other artists, such as composers, actors, and visual artists, work in the same way. Consciously or unconsciously, they create a structure in which all the elements of the work support their main theme.

Writing a story or poem or play may engage children more easily than an essay. Yet there is the challenge of giving structure to inspiration. Children need to let their fantasies flow and free-associate, but their work also needs to satisfy the rules of logic. Experience with our approach to essay writing can serve them well when it comes to their creative writing.

THE MECHANICS

Your child's range of ideas as well as his ability to express them and to feel emotional connections will help him to write organized essays and to give good reports. But two glitches can get in the way, even if the ideas and desire are there—that is, articulation and fine motor control.

Addressing these problems is essential because they can lead to or exacerbate other problems. A child's great ideas can get stymied because penmanship or speaking is so laborious. It's a little like six lanes of traffic flowing into a one-lane tunnel—all the traffic gets backed up. The child may either forget what he wants to say or write and/or get discouraged, anxious, or angry. Either way, he is likely to give up trying or get distracted by another activity—typical ways that children use to cope with frustration.

Articulation

We discussed initial verbal expressions in Chapter 8 on sounds. Single words gradually expand through conversation into phrases and sentences. (A related skill, making the connection between sounds and letters, a part of phonemic awareness, is also described there.) If we are working toward the goal of saying our thoughts logically, it makes sense that speaking clearly is the first step. If a child continues to have speech problems, school counselors or your pediatrician will probably be able to make a referral to a speech pathologist.

Improving Fine Motor Skills

A later mechanical step is physically putting thoughts down on paper. A child needs to develop fine motor skills to begin to express his ideas in writing. Articulation and writing skills are obviously not two sequential steps. Along with both, the child's powers of thinking, the core of expression, develop in remarkable ways.

Some children need a lot of practice just to manipulate a pencil and craft letters properly. Interestingly, some children have beautiful penmanship but labor over shaping each letter—it's almost as though they are drawing the letters rather than printing or eventually scripting them. They need more practice also.

An occupational therapist (either consulting to the child's classroom or to you directly) can explain the proper techniques for holding a pencil, and the skills can be practiced in many fun activities. In Chapter 10, we discussed how children go from scribbling in different colors and making free-form shapes, to geometric shapes, to drawing objects and interesting designs, and finally to starting on letters, initially putting one or two letters on a page.

Children whose fine motor skills are slow to develop can still get their ideas down on paper. Learning to type, which is usually easier than handwriting, is one option. Or if typing is equally frustrating and blocks ideas, the child can use a dictating machine. He dictates his ideas, listens to them, and then takes his time to write them out. Or while he's working on getting his penmanship up to speed, literally, you might even take dictation for him. If you hold the child to mastering penmanship first, the child will lose more than he gains because he will not be getting practice in expressing himself coherently.

Related neurological systems indirectly support the fine motor system. Activities that stress balance, coordination, and eye/hand practice—throwing, catching and kicking, walking on a balance beam, standing on one leg with eyes closed, climbing, moving through obstacle courses, or combinations of these (all discussed in Chapter 10)—will develop the different parts of the brain (the cerebellum as well as the frontal lobes) and strengthen planning and sequencing abilities. Again, be sure to work under the guidance of a good occupational therapist.

Here's a basic principle: when a fundamental ability—an aspect of the root system, such as fine motor control—is weak, you want to have infinite patience while the child practices the skill. It should be for short periods at a time and in a meaningful and fun way so the child doesn't get avoidant and negative. Like most of us, children prefer to do what comes easily and to avoid what is hard. It's not until the teen or adult years that someone can work on something that's difficult, consciously and volitionally, in order to achieve a goal. Young children don't think about the long-range future.

QUALITY VERSUS QUANTITY

A mistake we make in teaching children to write essays (as we said, many children get to college and still can't write a coherent essay) is to go for volume rather than quality. It's better to take a whole week with one short essay, if necessary, and make sure the child understands the structure—that is, he can diagram it and separate extraneous from relevant material—than to have the child write one essay after the next without that comprehension. If your child doesn't understand the basics, talk to the teacher and explain that he needs more time to finish an assignment. A grade-school child shouldn't spend more than an hour at a time working on an essay. If it will take four hours to get an assignment done and it's due the next day, ask the teacher if he can hand in an incomplete version or hand it in late. One solution to having more time may be for him to do every other essay assignment until he really understands the structure. If your child gets tempted or pressured just to get something down on paper, he will graduate from high school unable to do college work. It's better for a child to get a bad grade in fifth or sixth grade because he doesn't hand in all the work, if it means he's really learning how to write an essay, than to get by at this level but not be able to handle high school or college work. Grades in junior high don't matter much, but those in high school and college do. Given the importance of writing a logical essay or report for many careers, children need to learn this fundamental skill solidly.

Lively discussions with your child on his passionately held beliefs or wishes are the first step in helping him see how natural it is to prove a point. His desire to prove to you that he needs that extra piece of cake or deserves to go to the amusement park will provide much practice in making and proving a point—being logical. As we pointed out, this ability, nurtured by parents and others, entices the child into more complex discussions as he becomes older. When it comes time to write an essay, he will be more able to organize his thoughts quickly into an orderly diagram—either on paper or in his head—that succeeds in making his argument. This talent is one that can be nurtured in all children and improved upon even in the most gifted debaters and writers.

19

Mathematical Thinking
and Reasoning

Nowhere is our main message of an emotionally meaningful learning process more important than in mathematical thinking and reasoning. This area is very experience-based, and experiences involve emotions. As we discussed in Chapter 13, children use their emotions to get a sense of quantity well before they can count 1–2–3. For two-year-olds, "a lot" is a little more than they expect, and "a little" is less than they want. When a child has a choice between a big cookie and a little cookie, she usually wants the big one. She automatically makes the comparison because she is emotionally invested in the outcome. This is how she develops a sense of big versus little.

Math literacy also depends on all the thinking levels—the early levels of attention and regulation as well as complex problem-solving skills that involve pattern recognition. It relies heavily on a fundamental sense of causality (logical and multicausal thinking) and the development of comparative/gray-area thinking.

What about memory? If children can race through the multiplication tables easily, what does that really signify? Children who have good memories and can spew out these tables don't necessarily have a feel for math. In other words, they may not have a true sense of quantity and dimension if they haven't had experience with the real thing. Memorized facts can build on basic concepts but are not the main ingredient.

So, how should we teach those basic concepts if a child is finding them difficult? Once again, we return to multisensory, emotionally invested, motor-based experiences. We start at the child's developmental level (rather than age level), going back to whatever concept—addition, subtraction, multiplication, and division—gives the child trouble.

As remarkable as it sounds, we can cover all of these concepts—which are typically taught in the first four years of school—with the same kinds of experiences.

QUANTITY

Mathematical thinking builds heavily on visual-spatial processing (or in the case of blind children, touch) because they both involve understanding quantity and time. Children begin to understand quantity in their play with clay, cookies, blocks, or toy cars. This is where, as they enjoy themselves, they learn the concepts of "more" versus "less" and "big" versus "little." Say your child has made two lines of Matchbox cars—one with four cars and one with two. You can ask her to point to which line of cars is more and which is less (or which line is big and which is little). If she can't answer that question, ask which line she would like to have. If she loves cars, it will undoubtedly be the line with four cars. Explain to her that four is more than two so that line has more cars. Rearrange the cars and make two lines with five in one and a single one. Ask her again: which is more and which is less. Let her try arranging lines of more cars versus less. (To the grammarians reading this example, you are right. It should be fewer. Not to despair—you can introduce the difference between fewer versus less when the child is ready for comparative thinking.) Of course, cars are only one example. All kinds of play will strengthen a child's concept of quantity: building towers, baking cookies, drawing, or making sand castles.

In general, children don't fully understand this concept until they can build bridges between ideas (level six in our tree trunk)— that is, when they can answer basic why questions, typically, between the ages of three and four. Before this stage, though, children can still show preferences for more/less of what they want, and you can begin introducing the concept of quantity.

ADDITION AND SUBTRACTION

Once a child has the basic sense of more and less, it's on to step two: adding and subtracting. If a child has a problem with this, try out some play with blocks. With a "train" of four blocks and one of five blocks, you can ask your child which is bigger. If she picks the train with five blocks, you can add two blocks to the four blocks and ask, "Which one is bigger now?" Your child will probably choose the correct one. If not, start again with fewer blocks in each train, maybe one versus three. Once your child can answer correctly, you can ask, "Oh, how did it become bigger? What did I do?" The child will show you that you added blocks, and then you can point to the train with five blocks and ask, "Can you make this one as big as the other one? Can you make it even bigger?" And the child will add more blocks to make it bigger. Do the same thing with a tower or other forms.

When the child has the hang of addition, you can begin taking blocks away to make the tower or train smaller: "Let's see how small we can make it!" Now the child is experimenting with subtraction as well as addition, without using those terms. Ultimately, you want the child to take the lead, but you can do it first to show her how the process works.

NUMBERS

By this point, many children may have begun to count but haven't necessarily connected the numbers with specific objects. They haven't coordinated the "one" and the "two" with one block and two blocks. If this doesn't come easily, start simply with one, two, and three: "This is one block, now we have two, and now we have three." Arrange the objects in different shapes, adding and subtracting—but using numbers. If you have a tower of two blocks, ask the child, "If you add one onto the two, how many blocks do you have now?"

Then she counts: "One, two, three."

Then ask, "If we take one away, how many are there now?"

Your child counts: "One, two." And now your child is adding and subtracting with numbers. Let her make a tower with four blocks, then she adds/subtracts one and tells you how many there are. The changes in the tower should keep her interested.

You can progress to five, then ten, and even to twenty, all the while teaching your child the names of the numbers. Write out the number so she knows what the numbers one through ten look like. This way the child is seeing the number, hearing it, saying it, and manipulating it (in the form of whatever object she enjoys). For some children, this may take days or weeks—depending on how much difficulty they have and how much time parents spend on it—until they get it. When the child's interest lapses, pick an object that captures her interest again—whether it's dinosaurs, quarters, crackers, or raisins—that can reasonably be arranged into lines, towers, or other shapes. (It also helps to take a break. The next time, pick a different object.) There's nothing wrong with including an incentive, such as letting the child eat some of the raisins and then figuring out how many are left. This is the way to help children become emotionally invested in the basics of adding and subtracting.

CONSERVATION OF MATTER

Once the child has the basics of quantity, you can move on to the concept of the conservation of matter. (See also Chapter 13.) This means understanding that whether a single piece of clay, for instance, is stretched out into a snake or rolled up into a little ball, it is the same amount of clay. Play around with malleable objects, or water or juice in different shaped glasses, cotton batting in a ball or pulled apart as a beard. Start off with a tall glass and a wide glass with the same volume of liquid. Measure the contents in a measuring cup. You don't have to talk about cups or milliliters yet, but you can count the lines on the cup so that your child applies numbers to liquids to lay the foundation for later mathematical reasoning. Then take some liquid out of the tall glass. (Children who don't understand conservation always think the tall glass has more.) You can ask, "Which glass gives you more to drink?" and "Which one gives you less?" Again using the measuring cup, you can show the child that the tall glass has less. It's important for children to have an experiential understanding of these concepts before they learn formulas or memorize facts. Let your child experiment and discover objects whose shape she can change without changing the quantity or how the same amount of liquid looks different in different shaped glasses.

Once your child grasps these basics, you can introduce the idea of weight. Put a ball of clay and a clay snake on a scale so she sees that they weigh the same. Then add clay to the ball and just roll up the snake so that they now weigh different amounts. Ask, "Which one weighs more?" Let her pick them up and then weigh them. This introduces "lighter" versus "heavier."

DIVISION AND MULTIPLICATION

Gaining a sense of division and multiplication brings us back to the blocks or a Play-Doh pizza pie. Either a big cookie or even an actual pizza cut in four equal pieces works as well too (maybe even better from the child's point of view). "Okay, here we have this 'pizza,' and you want some and I want some. We both want to have about the same, so how are we going to do that?" Perhaps the child will figure out that cutting the shape in the middle gives each an equal amount. If the pieces are wildly unequal, ask the child if they are the same size for each of you. Now is the time to teach the word "half." Mom says to her daughter, "Okay, now I have half of the whole thing and you have half. Half is when we divide it into two equal parts."

Next, start with four pieces. Ask the child to distribute them equally. Say the child takes three pieces and gives Mom one. "Wait! That's not the same—who has more?"

The child looks at the pieces and says, "I've got more. I want more!"

Mom can ask, "Okay, but just for fun, can we have the same, just for a minute, then you get to have more?" to see if her daughter can really divide up the pieces equally.

Some children will get this right away, especially if they can already count. If not, eventually, by figuring it out—or just by chance—the child will divide the pieces up equally. Then you want to see if she can replicate with blocks or something else she is interested in.

For more understanding of division, you can bring in more characters who want to have some of the pie too—maybe stuffed animals or other family members. "How can you and I and Teddy Bear and Daddy have the same amount? Show me how much to give to each of us." The child can experiment with blocks or drawing lines with a dull knife on a cookie until everyone gets one piece.

From there, it is easy to explain that when there are four pieces and everyone gets one, then everyone has a quarter of the pie. A child doesn't have to use these terms right away. The idea is just to give her an experiential preview of the concept and to help her learn the word "division." She understands what "divide" means because she's done it herself. You can play with the concept—using different objects, including types of food (maybe the child can even help divide the food at the dinner table). Keep the numbers low, under five, until the child has mastered the concept.

The same process applies to learning multiplication. Here's Mom working with her son. He can already count to ten easily, so she asks, "Okay, we've got me and you, and we each want one piece of the cookie. How many pieces are we going to need?"

He figures that out easily: "Two pieces."

Then she says, "Okay, but now we each want two pieces. How many are we going to need?"

Suppose her son says, "I don't know!"

She can then say, "Well, give us each two and see how many there are when you do that." He counts out one, two, three, four. Next, she brings in Teddy Bear and Dinosaur and starts over. Each of them gets two pieces and again the total is four. Now she adds Teddy in with her and her son so that there are three of them. She goes through one piece for each of them, then two for each and three for each. Once he can do this, she explains, "There's a word for what we're doing—it's called 'multiplying.' There are three of us, and each one is getting three pieces, and the way we describe that is 'three times three.'" The word "times" in this context will be new for a young child. He may not quite understand it yet, but he gets the experience of multiplying—of giving a certain amount to a certain number of people. Three objects given to three people will always equal nine objects.

As we continue with these multiplication and division exercises, we can bring in other terms, such as "percentage," if the child is quick verbally, and then we can use the terms "50 percent," "25 percent," or "100 percent." Again, the idea isn't for a child to understand percentages or fractions at this point but simply to hear the words and experience what percentage feels like. When the Sidwell kindergartners read the labels on food and compared the amounts of sodium and protein, the weights are in both whole numbers and percent of the daily allowance. They would not have known how to figure the percentage, but they would see that the more sodium in a product, the higher the percentage of sodium. This basic cause and effect relationship is part of logical thinking.

This process, of course, will be played out over many weeks. Once the child understands simple addition and subtraction, conservation of matter, and counting—in both visual and auditory form—you can add on multiplication and division and play a little bit with fractions and percentages as described above, using real objects of interest to the child. Once that understanding is established, a child can memorize her multiplication tables or some of the simple math facts so she doesn't have to use her fingers. But it's better early on for children to use their fingers or objects such as blocks until they get it.

VISUAL AND VERBAL MATHEMATICAL SKILLS

Some children have an easy time with numbers and can learn to add and subtract, and even divide and multiply, fairly easily, but they have a hard time with word problems because of a language or sequencing problem. They have trouble transferring what they hear to what they see, that is, the words into numbers. Others are just the opposite—they're better with word problems but have a harder time dealing with visual symbols. Once children have mastered the basics in an experiential context, as above, then it's important that they become facile with both the verbal and the visual forms of math.

To help a child shift back and forth between verbal and visual mathematical thinking, practice is key. If a child has trouble with word problems, play it out. Dad got the two dolls Susie and Polly (action figures work too), wrote down a simple word problem, and read it together with his child, "If we want to give Susie two pebbles and Polly two, how many pebbles do we need all together?" Dad put a slip of paper with two pebbles on it in front of Susie and did the same for Polly. He asked his daughter to write down the number of pebbles on each slip. Then he wrote out, "2 + 2 = ?" and asked, "How many do we need?" His daughter was able to write down "4," but if she had not, he could have given her options, say, the numbers 4, 5, and 3 and asked her to circle the correct one. Finishing up, Dad asked his daughter, who had good fine motor control, if she could write out the whole problem: "2 + 2 = 4." This type of exercise lets a child break down the question into its basic logical parts and build up from these pieces to get the answer.

The idea is to bring the verbal statement alive visually and then represent it on a piece of paper. A child who doesn't sequence well may need further work on executive functioning skills or motor planning and sequencing (addressed in the next chapter). If you work on the verbal and the visual aspects of math from the beginning, then math can strengthen language and language can strengthen math. Math can also strengthen visual processing and vice versa.

Finally, as with language skills, practice in mathematical thinking and reasoning needs to be individualized so that, when challenged, the child experiences at least a 70 percent success rate. If necessary, slow down the process or return to an earlier stage so that the child develops mastery at each level.

20

Dorothy Littell Greco

Organizational Skills

Many children are diagnosed with an "organizational learning disability." The term serves for a whole host of challenges, but essentially it includes problems with attention, sequencing, and organizing. Together these abilities create executive functioning (briefly discussed in Chapter 11). Having strong executive functioning means that you can see both the forest and the trees and have the discipline to carry out a project to completion. It means seeing the big picture, identifying the details you must work with, figuring out the steps, and staying at the task until you successfully execute a plan. Children who have difficulties in this area are weak in one or more of the needed skills.

Executive functioning, perhaps more than any other skill, depends on the strength of the tree trunk. The higher a child's level of thinking, the better his ability will be for focusing, sequencing, organizing, and staying on task. If a child has climbed through the higher thinking levels, he can, for instance, reflect on whether he should watch TV before finishing his homework and what the steps are to get the homework done. If he decides to turn on the TV and neglect his homework, it's a conscious decision. It isn't due to poor organizational abilities. At the reflective thinking level, he is in charge of his actions and his underlying emotions and motivations. He can think them through so that he understands the consequences.

On the other hand, if he has poor organizational abilities, he wouldn't think it through and instead would make a snap judgment based on no consideration of the amount of homework. He would say to himself: "It's only 30 minutes. No sweat. I've got the whole night to get my homework done." A child's level of interest and emotional investment are as important here as with all the other branches. It is rare to see a child who wants a particular privilege or treat remain too disorganized to keep coming back to ask for it. When the stakes are high, most children can stay focused and be disciplined. But most of life is not driven by strong desires. Unfortunately for all of us, the mundane demands attention and discipline too.

The question is how to get your child to attend to and then organize the less than interesting stuff. Below are some practical suggestions. As you can see, to some degree executive functioning is an amalgam of many of the skills and abilities that we have talked about throughout the book. These work only if the beginning thinking levels are fairly solid. If your child is still struggling with attention and engagement, with participating in a rhythmic flow of communication or with basic problem-solving, watch for those lapses and go back to earlier chapters to help the child develop these. Then use the ideas below to work toward improving executive functioning.

The previous chapters on the senses contain many games to improve needed skills. For instance, Chapter 13 on visual-spatial processing suggests games for observing details at the basic thinking levels and, building on that at the higher level of problem-solving, for recognizing patterns. Then, to give the games added emotional weight, you can be very interested in your child's opinion about what he sees, which marbles are his favorite, and which ones he doesn't like, all with enthusiastic responses from you.

Performing complicated rhythmical movements helps to develop sequencing skills. As discussed earlier (Chapter 10), a product called the Interactive Metronome gives computer feedback for rhythmic activity, such as clapping one's hands or moving one's feet. Our research has shown that it improves academic skills as well as attention. In Chapter 9 on mastering sounds, Isabelle, the singer who had trouble sight-reading, was introduced to a number of games that developed speed and dexterity in sequencing skills. She watched a blinking light to note when patterns changed. She matched visual symbols with verbal directions (also symbols).

To incorporate higher levels of thinking—comparative, gray-area, and reflective—try debates in which each person has a short period of time to defend his point of view. The process starts by having the child decide what the big debate issue is. Then each person gets two minutes to prepare an argument and one minute to argue it, or whatever time the debaters think is reasonable.

In summary, to develop executive functioning, help your child practice the individual skill(s) that need boosting. Along with setting up exercises as close as possible to the real situations the child will confront at school—essay tests, math problems, and debating—also work on the fundamentals. The stronger the child's basic thinking skills, the stronger his organizational skills will be.

Simply put, a person does not acquire real knowledge by simply listening to or reading something. The basic thinking levels, the developmental process, need to be in place so that there is a mind ready to receive and organize the information.

SEEING THE BIG PICTURE

For a child with problems organizing schoolwork, the first step is to fit it into the context of a child's evening. Homework is a very common example. The big picture is what the child has to do that evening, one item of which is homework. A useful tool at home is a blank sheet—either a blackboard or paper, with chalk or marker, whatever he is comfortable with—so that he can create a map. On the sheet he lists what he will do during the evening, such as chores, family time, dinner, and homework. (Fortunately, with the Internet, many school systems now post homework or test assignments.)

Next to each item on the list, he marks down how much he wants to do the activity, using a scale of zero to ten. Next to that, he indicates the likelihood that he'll do it on his own—will do it, doesn't want to do it, needs physical help to do it, needs support to do it, or needs help with facts or research. The response of "doesn't want to do it" often reflects an insecurity about the task, which may relate to worry about his ability to carry it out—or it could simply be a boring task, such as washing dishes. If a parent and child talk through the task, those feelings and reasons will come out, and together they can work on raising his confidence or discussing why something must be done.

Last, the child estimates how much time each task will take. The parent sometimes needs to interject a note of reality here. ("No, even though you wish the essay would take only fifteen minutes to write, you remember how last week's assignment took a lot more.")

Then parent and child can prioritize the activities and negotiate the order in which they are to be completed. When he does A (a chore) and B (a math assignment), he then gets to do E, which might be talking to his friend for a certain amount of time; when he does F (his reading assignment) and G (walking the dog), he gets to do H, which might be playing a video game for awhile.

Just writing down the list is good practice. He has looked at the big picture and seen where his homework fits in. He has outlined his tasks, his interest level, and his likelihood of doing them. This analysis takes knowing himself and helps him to be a reflective thinker.

The more the child can accomplish on his own, the better, but this may be a gradual process. At the start, parents do what is needed so that he reaches his goals. They can initially set it up so that he reports to them or they come in and check on him. Depending on his "likelihood" response, they may even need to sit with him while he does certain homework. By making the chart, his choices are now deliberate—it's no longer, "I forgot"—though he may still get off track at first. Friendly support to finish the last three math problems so he can call a friend may be the needed boost. Or external incentives, such as extra time on a favorite activity, may be needed to get some of the least desired things done. This way, the positive feelings about the more desirable activities get transferred to and combined with the less desirable items. Parents can view their job as helping their son stay organized so that he gets to do the fun things on the list.

Practicing organization can be useful for any kind of task, not just homework. It will help with anything that requires sequencing, focus, and self-regulation, particularly where there is mixed motivation on the child's part. The child can list the steps required for writing thank-you notes for presents, practicing the piano, or taking care of a pet. Getting ready for school in the morning so he's not late is often a big issue for disorganized children. The big picture is how to organize the morning so that he gets to school on time without extra stress. This could include what time to get up, what to have for breakfast, what clothes to wear, and when to fill up the backpack. The child can identify some of these as "desirable," others as "a drag," and arrange them accordingly. Along with reduced chaos and stress in the morning, the child will see how planning works.

With enough practice in writing down each step and organizing what has to be done, a child will begin to feel in more control of the bigger picture, and the process will become second nature. The habit of making a plan, such as for doing homework, will eventually become more and more automatic. This approach will gradually generalize to other tasks and obligations.

MOTIVATION AND PRACTICE

If an activity is easy for us, we're usually happy to do it anytime. If it's hard, we tend to avoid it. Children, especially, operate on that principle—they do what's easy and fun and avoid what isn't. It's not a question of "good students" and "bad students." There are kids who learn reading and writing easily and enjoy school, and others who have a harder time with these activities and so dislike school. So our goal is to increase the child's interest and skill so that academic activities become, if not as much fun as riding a bike or playing with friends, then at least easy enough so that the child won't avoid them.

Children start off with very different sequencing and organizing abilities—some children will be stronger in one sensory or motor system than another. Some will be good at verbal sequencing and will write good essays but are weak at motor sequencing and will not be able to learn a new dance or new sport easily. Others will be just the reverse. So the key is practice in the area that is hardest for the child. Improvement in the weak areas will help the child's overall sequencing and organizing and thus strengthen his executive functioning and his ability to take on an academic project.

In previous chapters (see Chapters 10, 17, and 18), we addressed how to start with emotionally meaningful topics when helping children to practice skills—whether expressing ideas in writing or speaking and solving math problems. We all have a natural tendency to be organized around subjects that are important to us. Strategies to incorporate this principle include helping a child find a point of view he connects with or one he can argue with, such as the teacher's (always a good way to get an oppositional and negative child to stir up his emotions and to stay organized).

If the area is math, organize the math around an interest. Sports are good for that because they involve scoring and numbers. But here we are not talking about simply adding a successful three-point shot to the total. You have to start with a bigger goal. For instance, if your daughter is a basketball fan, you two can watch a game and figure out your own process for determining the most valuable player. To start, you and your daughter can discuss the different factors that are important and how important they are relative to each other. The MVP process can be as simple or complicated as your daughter wants and can handle arithmetically. Maybe she decides to look at points, assists, and blocks. Points accumulate as usual, and assists and blocks each get one-half point. The player with the most points wins. (You can get deeper into fractions if she has been introduced to them already.) She can make a big chart with the players' names down one side and the criteria on the top. She needs to keep all the criteria straight; decide how she will record each event (e.g., does she record the actual points earned or the number of baskets scored?); and track who is doing what. When the game is over, the points added up, and the winner announced, you and she can reflect on whether the referees did a good job. Do you both agree that the winner played the best game? Were there other factors that were important but not included? Would they have changed the result? Would you design and execute your system the same way again? This is but one example of executive functioning practice that can be fun: plan the big picture, stay focused, watch the details, sequence the events, do the math, and then evaluate or reflect on the process.

PRACTICE IN FOLLOWING DIRECTIONS

Most school activities can be practiced. But if they are only practiced at school, a child who experiences difficulty may not get enough practice.

Let's start with following directions—a problem in school for children who can't sequence but one that is not often identified. Children may not know they have trouble with this or may not want to tell you they do. If you simply ask your child what directions and tasks are difficult for him to follow—such as knowing the assignment, keeping his desk organized, lining up numbers in complicated long division or multiplication problems (which requires fine motor skills as well as remembering math steps)—he may not 'fess up, or he may not have really seen the problem as such.

If you suspect this is a problem or the teacher has noticed it, over the course of a few weeks you and your child can play the "what's up for tomorrow game." This can begin with simply sharing what each of you is doing tomorrow. You establish a rhythm—talking about things that are fun, talking about things that just need to be done, and eventually getting to things that are problems. Son Billy talks about playing dodgeball at recess and how, when he is in the middle, he knows which thrower is really good, so he'll keep farther away from him. And Mom talks about going to the grocery store after work to buy food for dinner, including the special can of soup that Billy likes. And Billy says he has to hand in the permission slip to go on the field trip, and Mom asks him what he does to help him remember because she has an important phone call that she needs to remember. At first, in talking about the events of the next day, Billy probably won't volunteer that he has trouble, for instance with following all the instructions for doing art projects, but eventually he will. Then it is problem-solving time.

Whatever problems with directions emerge, you can create enjoyable ways to practice. For example, dissecting the instructions for the art project may require a blackboard so Billy can list all the individual steps—getting the smock, the paints, brushes, and paper; washing the brushes; and hanging up his picture to dry. Are there any of these tasks that he doesn't like to do? (It's easy to forget to do what you don't like.) Playing out what happens when he forgets his smock or leaves the brushes on the table, "yikes, what a mess," will bring emotional content to the reasons for following the instructions.

If your child enjoys them, good old games such as Simon Says give general practice at following instructions. You start with one command ("Simon says touch your toes"), and then advance to two commands, then three, four, and five in a row ("Simon says touch your toes, touch your elbows, touch your nose, walk ten steps, then walk backward five steps and sideways two steps"). At first give slow directions and then move to faster ones. Once the child gets the hang of it, include a friend or a sibling and make it a competition. Let your child be Simon sometimes.

If the sequencing problems are in reading comprehension or writing, remember Jack in Chapter 9. Your child can practice questions with two ideas in them, such as, "Who was the best scientist during the Revolutionary War period, besides Benjamin Franklin?" You can give points for the proper interpretation of the question and provide rewards, depending on how many points the child earns. Rather than writing a whole essay, the child can outline a subject, such as, "Why is this computer game better than that computer game?" The child can come up with a thesis and then an organized list of arguments, in order to get the hang of the structure. Ultimately, he should be able to do this in just a few minutes. From there, the child can actually write out whole sentences and paragraphs to put the "meat on the bones" of the essay.

Treasure hunts with a combination of verbal and visual directions, discussed in earlier chapters, are also a great way to practice these skills, as are obstacle courses to help develop mental and motor sequencing skills. Parents' being a little "disorganized" or "lazy" is another way. For example, if your child wants you to take him to the local pool, ask him what he needs to do to get ready. "Hmmm . . . what do you need?" Let your child figure it out: pool hours, bathing suit, goggles, towel, sunscreen, and so forth. It's an older-age iteration of the Socrates moment in Floortime, when you challenge the child to expand his thinking. The child, who is now motivated by his own interests, will become a good sequencer. A little lower on the fun scale are household chores, good for both teaching family "citizenship" and learning to sequence and organize.

A good way to tell if a child is organized—whether in terms of writing an essay, doing math problems, playing tennis, or participating in any other activity—is when the child can teach the activity to you. When children can do this, they've really mastered it. Our son Jake, who works with children with special needs, came up with the idea of having the child teach his parents how to play whatever game the child enjoys, even if it is one he has made up. In this situation, the child is motivated to develop sequencing skills because he gets to be the boss and because he likes the activity. Complementary to this technique is to ask your child what he would do if he were the boss: how would he run the house? How would he organize the evening? What would he have you do because you're always making him do things? Not only will you be amazed at your child's thoughts, but you will see how well he can sequence when he is involved in the process.

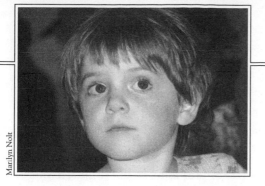

21

The Learning Tree in Conclusion
The Sidwell Friends Native Americans and Colonists Project

By Richard Lodish, Ed.D., with Susanne Saunders

A good example of how higher-level thinking skills bolster learning took place with the third- and fourth-graders at the Sidwell Friends School. What is especially important in this example is the emotional involvement, reflection, and planning that occurred. These students had quite a challenge. Even though, as their teacher Susan Saunders said, they were "used to unconventional lessons, high drama, and a certain degree of unpredictability that keeps them wondering what might come next," they would not have anticipated the situation they faced.

Drawing on diverse resources, the third- and fourth-graders had spent a few months learning about different American Indian nations and customs. They had made intricate cradle boards from chamois and beads; leather pouches that were punched and laced by hand; and travois, a two-poled frame drawn by horses. Classroom shelves displayed their hard work as well as real Indian artifacts. Along with the actual and replicated Indian cultural objects, the children learned the proper handling of ceremonial items, carefully respecting the "no handling" policy for more delicate objects, such as hand-carved kachina dolls and smudge fans made from bird wings, as well as the most admired artifact, a beautifully painted arrow designed to ensure buffalo fertility and thus tribal prosperity.

One morning, the principal came to the classroom and announced that a water pipe had burst in another part of the school. Apologetically, he explained that he would need to use part of the classroom, one of the biggest in the school, for emergency storage of some large boxes. Students, teachers, and principal then moved chairs and desks aside to accommodate the temporary materials. Then the students settled down into their newly confined space.

After awhile, another teacher appeared at the door with a related announcement. She had to evacuate her room to allow for the repair of the water pipe. Her students were in the midst of an important lesson that had to be finished, and she asked if they could use some of the class workspace. The third- and fourth-graders, somewhat begrudgingly, gave up their desks, bunched up as they were, and retreated to their gathering space on the floor. Again, they settled in. But when the morning snack arrived and had to be divided with the visitors, a few complaints began to circulate. Many, though, were still pleased to share, as the visiting students were their friends.

As the morning proceeded, the visiting students, who were also studying Native Americans, noticed the cultural objects displayed and were suddenly intrigued. And then something amazing happened. The visitors not only picked up the ceremonial objects in a disrespectful manner, but they actually loaded some of the more desirable ones into bins to take back to their own classroom for display. Gone from the shelf were the sacred smudge fans, the delicate kachinas, and the prized arrow. The teacher did not object because these were school property and intended for both classes. Her bewildered students looked to her for guidance. In the midst of this, the visiting teachers spied the children's handmade replicas and let their children scoop them up too. Some of the homeroom students positioned themselves near special items as if to defend them. Others on the side raised their fists in protest. The visitors, rather pleased with their new trophies, clapped each other on the back in a congratulatory manner. At just that moment, the principal returned to say that the water pipe was repaired and all were to march back to their own room immediately. Unfortunately for the homeroom students, the timing was perfect. Their treasures were callously carted away by the plunderers, while they were left stranded and shocked in a cramped classroom still half-filled with boxes.

The clamoring began immediately. Although all were outraged by the mauling of the sacred objects, they disputed what to do next: Some spoke for tolerance and a wish to clean up the room; others were incensed and wanted to demand their belongings back. But the assault on the room had not quite ended. As the children considered sending a delegation to express the feelings of the class, the other teachers came to the door with a few pieces of the students' handiwork and with one of the prized possessions. Along with these items came an admission. When they hauled the ill-gotten goods back to the class, a precious kachina doll was dropped and one arm broke off. It was completely accidental. There in the box, the broken doll lay among the returned goods.

This was too much for some. Once the door closed, a visibly angered group of boys laid out a plan to raid the other classroom during recess and wreck some things there. War was about to break out.

The teachers asked the children to sit, try to calm themselves, and listen to some important information. One of the teachers then offered a confession. The entire episode was prearranged—from the ruse of the broken water pipe to the pillaging of their work, which had been preselected for maximum impact. She asked that they blame her for the anger and confusion that they had experienced and not the other class. Then she asked them to think about why she put them through the discomfort.

The children immediately knew the answer—their next study section, European settlements in North America. And they quickly came to agreement on what caused them the deepest distress. As their teacher described,

> They felt invisible as a group and confused by the seeming arrogance of our visitors. They were intimidated by those who were in authority. They were appalled at the evident disregard for our traditions and taboos. They felt helpless to prevent disrespectful handling of items that were particularly meaningful to them. They were powerless to prevent the removal of cherished objects.

They drew parallels between the morning's events and those that enveloped native nations, from their initial welcome of the other students, to feeling intruded upon with the reduced space and shared snacks, and finally to anger as the things they cared about were brashly stripped from them.

Echoing back the students' comments and reactions, the teachers helped them identify the peacemakers, warmongers, and undecided among them. They discussed different approaches by gender. They asked the students how they could emotionally distance themselves from the events of the morning and use the simulation to understand their studies. They framed the experience in terms of the historical perspective, and they framed it in terms of personal reactions. They asked the children how it made them feel from an emotional point of view and what they needed to process the events.

The answer of the majority—to be invaders.

Through collaboration, the teachers concocted a logistical/scheduling dilemma that would land the students in the classroom of the original invaders. Before the "assault," the new invaders analyzed what worked for the original ones and what didn't. They knew exactly what they were doing. And so, with many, many weeks passing to let heightened feelings quiet, these third- and fourth-graders descended upon the original invading class, in much the same manner as they had experienced. Eventually the invaded classroom did see through the ruse, but it was sufficiently successful that the invaded class too became angry.

These new invaders then had the opposite situation and set of feelings to think through. With lengthy discussions on fairness, rights, aggression, belief systems as evident from actions, and the demonstration of power, the children developed an understanding of historical events and an understanding of their own reactions, be it a desire to plunder or to negotiate. Wrote their teacher,

> The basic unfairness of our transactions touched a deep chord within many, and they were able to see clearly how they had benefited from the encounter. Although they felt some sympathy with our "victims," they didn't, for the most part, let it interfere with their actions. Because they had previously been victimized, they felt they were, in some sense, justified in being callous toward others. They remarked on the differences between individuals and how far they were willing to go to secure personal gain. They explored the pleasure inherent in feeling "wealthy," more "knowledgeable" about what was going on, and clear about their goals.

Any child, with or without learning problems, could learn from this experience. However, the experience is not for all children. The crucial element is the emotional level of the children. When a similar situation of creating haves and have-nots was tried in a school with children who were not yet as sophisticated, the children felt truly abused by the other students. They were not able to step back, reflect on the situation, and understand that it was a simulation.

Further Reading

Ayres, A. Jean. *Sensory Integration and the Child: 25th Anniversary Edition*. Los Angeles: Western Psychological Services, 2005.

Note: It is important to separate Ayres's clinical observations about sensory differences from her emphasis on the value of the vestibular system to organize the sensory system. Even those who disagree with Ayres's organizational theory should make use of her very astute clinical observations.

Brazelton, T. Berry, and Joshua Sparrow. *Touchpoints 3–6*. Cambridge, MA: Da Capo Press (A Merloyd Lawrence Book), 2001.

Escalona, Sybille. *The Roots of Individuality*. Chicago: Aldine Press, 1968.

Fraiberg, Selma. *The Magic Years*. New York: Scribner's, 1996.

Furth, H., and Harry Wachs. *Thinking Goes to School*. New York: Oxford University Press, 1974.

Greenspan, Stanley I., and Diane Lewis. *The Affect-Based Learning Curriculum*. 2nd ed. Bethesda, MD: Interdisciplinary Council on Developmental and Learning Disorders, 2005.

Greenspan, Stanley I., and Serena Wieder. *Engaging Autism*. Cambridge, MA: Da Capo Press (A Merloyd Lawrence Book), 2006.

Greenspan, Stanley I., with Beryl Benderly. *The Growth of the Mind and the Endangered Origins of Intelligence*. Cambridge, MA: Da Capo Press (A Merloyd Lawrence Book), 1997.

Greenspan, Stanley I., with Jacob Greenspan. *Overcoming ADHD: Helping Your Child Become Calm, Engaged, and Focused, Without a Pill.* Cambridge, MA: Da Capo Press (A Merloyd Lawrence Book), 2009.

Greenspan, Stanley I., with Nancy B. Lewis. *Building Healthy Minds: The Six Experiences That Create Intelligence and Emotional Growth in Babies and Young Children.* Cambridge, MA: Da Capo Press (A Merloyd Lawrence Book), 1999.

Holt, John. *How Children Learn.* Cambridge, MA: Da Capo Press (A Merloyd Lawrence Book), 1967, 1995.

Piaget, Jean. *The Origins of Intelligence in Children.* New York: Oxford University Press, 1952.

Index

About the Authors

Nancy Thorndike Greenspan is a writer and former economist. *The Learning Tree* is the fourth book on which she has collaborated with her husband, Stanley Greenspan. The mother of three children, she was, with Stanley's guidance and encouragement, the original Floortime mom. Mrs. Greenspan has also written *The End of the Certain World*, a biography of Nobel laureate and quantum physics pioneer Max Born.

Stanley I. Greenspan, M.D. (1941–2010), who died shortly after finishing his work on this book, was a clinical professor of psychiatry and pediatrics at George Washington University Medical School and chair of the Interdisciplinary Council on Developmental and Learning Disorders. He was also a practicing child psychiatrist; founding president of Zero to Three: The National Center for Infants, Toddlers, and Families; and a supervising child psychoanalyst at the Washington Psychoanalytic Institute. Earlier, he had been director of the Mental Health Study Center and the Clinical Infant Development Program at the National Institute of Mental Health.

Dr. Greenspan, whose methods guide the care of infants and children with developmental and emotional problems throughout the world, was the author or editor of more than forty books and one hundred articles. His many influential works, which have been translated into more than a dozen languages, include *The Growth of the Mind* (with Beryl Benderly); *Building Healthy Minds* (with Nancy Lewis); *The Challenging Child* and *Playground Politics* (with Jacqueline Salmon); *Overcoming ADHD*; *First Feelings* (with Nancy Thorndike Greenspan); *Engaging Autism* and *The Child with Special Needs* (both with Serena Wieder); *Infancy and Early Childhood*; and *Developmentally Based Psychotherapy*.

Among Dr. Greenspan's many national honors are the American Psychiatric Association's Ittleson Prize, its highest award for child psychiatry research; the American Orthopsychiatry's Ittleson Prize for pioneering contributions to American mental health (he was the only individual to receive both Ittleson prizes); and the Edward A. Strecker Award for outstanding contributions to American psychiatry. Please see www.StanleyGreenspan.com.